How Did Employee Ownership Firms Weather the Last Two Recessions?

How Did Employee Ownership Firms Weather the Last Two Recessions?

Employee Ownership, Employment Stability, and Firm Survival: 1999–2011

Fidan Ana Kurtulus
Douglas L. Kruse

2017

W.E. Upjohn Institute for Employment Research
Kalamazoo, Michigan

Library of Congress Cataloging-in-Publication Data

Names: Kurtulus, Fidan Ana, author. | Kruse, Douglas, author.
Title: How did employee ownership firms weather the last two recessions? :
   employee ownership, employment stability, and firm survival: 1999–2011 / Fidan
   Ana Kurtulus, Douglas L. Kruse.
Description: Kalamazoo, Michigan : W.E. Upjohn Institute for Employment Research,
   2016. | Includes bibliographical references and index.
Identifiers: LCCN 2016049037 | ISBN 9780880995252 (pbk. : alk. paper) | ISBN
   0880995254 (pbk. : alk. paper) | ISBN 9780880995269 (hardcover : alk. paper) |
   ISBN 0990995262 (hardcover : alk. paper)
Subjects: LCSH: Employee ownership—United States. | Management—Employee
   participation—United States. | Unemployment—United States. | Business failures—
   United States. | Recessions—United States.
Classification: LCC HD5660.U5 K87 2016 | DDC 338.6/90973090511–dc23
LC record available at https://lccn.loc.gov/2016049037.

© 2017
W.E. Upjohn Institute for Employment Research
300 S. Westnedge Avenue
Kalamazoo, Michigan 49007-4686

Cover design by Carol A.S. Derks.
Index prepared by Laura Dewey.
Printed in the United States of America.
Printed on recycled paper.

Fidan dedicates this book to her husband, Travis,
her son, John Aydin, and her parents, Shirley and Ercis.

For Doug, all roads lead to Lisa.

not just a question of higher
productivity, but of investment
does it get at that
long-term angle

investment in esop
firms better
share repurchases lower

Contents

Figures

Tables

Acknowledgments

We would like to acknowledge the tremendous ongoing support in many ways from our colleague Joseph Blasi, who has provided both valuable encouragement and substantive advice throughout the development of this book. We are extremely grateful to Richard Freeman, who has given us detailed comments as discussant at several conferences and workshops where we presented parts of this research, and who continues to be an extraordinary mentor. The first encouragement to transform this research into a book came from Steve Woodbury, and we are very thankful to him for his mentorship and support. We are also very grateful to our colleagues at the Upjohn Institute for Employment Research, especially Kevin Hollenbeck and the editorial staff, for their support throughout the creation of this book, and to the three anonymous referees for their helpful comments on the manuscript. We are very appreciative of the grant support from the Upjohn Institute for this book project.

We also acknowledge the scholars in the Beyster Symposiums, Kelso Workshops, Allied Social Sciences Meetings, International Association for the Economics of Participation Meetings, and the London School of Economics Centre for Economic Performance/National Institute for Economics Research Workshop, where these results have been presented. The scholars—too numerous to mention by name here—have provided many useful comments on the substance of the research and a supportive environment for exploring the myriad of issues around employee ownership. We present some results from analysis of the U.S. General Social Survey, conducted by the National Opinion Research Center, and are grateful to the Employee Ownership Foundation for their grant to the University of Chicago supporting the Shared Capitalism Module of the General Social Survey.

Fidan Ana Kurtulus worked on parts of this book while at Harvard Law School, Rutgers University School of Management and Labor Relations, Boston University Economics Department, and Harvard Kennedy School of Government, and she is grateful for their hospitality. She received grant support for portions of the research that went into this book from the Cabral Fellowship, Beyster Fellowship, Huber Fellowship, and Rutgers University Senior Fellowship, and she thanks them for this support. She is also grateful for the ongoing support of her colleagues at the University of Massachusetts Amherst, where she is an associate professor, and for the support of Jed DeVaro, who has been her mentor since her days as a graduate student. Above all, Fidan is thankful for the love and support of her husband, Travis Hinson; her parents, Shirley and Ercis Kurtulus; and her son, John Aydin Hinson, who was born during the final stages of writing this book.

Doug Kruse greatly values the ongoing support of his colleagues at the Rutgers University School of Management and Labor Relations, where he is a professor, in particular Dean James Hayton of the Rutgers School of Management and Labor Relations, former Dean Sue Schurman, former Dean David Finegold, Associate Dean Adrienne Eaton, former Associate Dean Paula Voos, and Department Chairs David Allen and Lisa Schur. He worked on this book as a Beyster Faculty Fellow at Rutgers University. Finally, Doug continues to be grateful for the tremendous love and support of his wife, Lisa Schur; his parents, Ruth and Lowen Kruse; his sister and her family, Jorika, Barry, Lauren, and Kiera Stockwell; and his extended family, Janet Schur and Michelle and Madison Link.

1
Introduction

Trends and Prior Evidence

Employee ownership is a situation in which employees have an ownership stake in the firm where they work, through holdings of firm stock. It is a channel through which employees share in the profits of the firm and can vote on important firm decisions and otherwise have increased participation in workplace decisions. The focus of this book is on broad-based employee ownership—that is, ownership of stock not just by top-level managers but by workers at all levels of a firm's hierarchy. The past several decades have witnessed growth in broad-based employee participation in the financial performance of firms, both in the United States and in other advanced countries.

WHY DO WE CARE?

There are four broad sources of interest in employee ownership:

1) **Increased economic performance.** Since employee ownership shares the overall pie with employees of the firm, participation in employee ownership can motivate employees to work harder to increase the size of the pie, primarily through increased productivity. Employee ownership can thus alleviate principal-agent problems in the workplace. By tying worker pay to profits, the incentives of workers and owners can become aligned so that productivity-reducing conflict is minimized and productivity-enhancing cooperation and innovation are encouraged. Better outcomes can occur through higher worker effort, lower absenteeism and turnover, and greater worker commitment and willingness to share information and cooperate with management. There should be especially strong effects if employee ownership is combined

1

with employee participation in decisions (combining "residual control" with "residual returns") (Holmstrom and Milgrom 1994; Jensen and Meckling 1992; Milgrom and Roberts 1990; Prendergast 2002).

2) **Greater job security and firm survival.** Employee ownership may enhance firm survival and employment stability, through greater compensation flexibility and higher productivity. If so, this can help decrease unemployment and increase macroeconomic stability in the overall economy, creating positive externalities that can justify supportive public policy.

3) **More-broadly shared prosperity.** Employee ownership can broaden access to capital income and broaden the distribution of income and wealth. The notion of workers sharing in firm profits has historical roots in the infancy of U.S. capitalism. The founders of the United States believed that broad sharing in ownership and economic rewards was vital to a thriving democracy (Blasi, Freeman, and Kruse 2013). Albert Gallatin, before becoming U.S. Treasury secretary under Thomas Jefferson, instituted a profit-sharing plan in 1795 at his Pennsylvania Glass Works, with the belief that such a system was important for the newly developing U.S. democracy. Broadening the distribution of wealth was a key reason for the creation of employee stock ownership plans (ESOPs) by Louis Kelso and their institutionalization in the Employee Retirement Income Security Act of 1974 (ERISA), spearheaded by Sen. Russell Long of Louisiana.

4) **Lower labor-management conflict and higher quality of work life.** Employee ownership may help to create a more harmonious work site, with less labor-management conflict because of increased alignment of incentives. Employees may also benefit from increased job security and control of their work lives. To the extent that employee ownership increases employee participation in workplace decisions, this may also help to strengthen democracy by increasing employees' civic skills and interest in participating in politics, as argued by the political scientist Carole Pateman (1970).

Because of the above sources of interest, a number of countries give tax incentives to promote employee ownership. The European Union (EU) highlighted employee ownership and profit sharing in its four reports from 1991 to 2008 known as the PEPPER (Promotion of Employee Participation in Profits and Enterprise Results) Reports. It called on member states to promote participation by employed persons in profits and enterprise performance. Employee ownership can improve individual firm performance, which provides a rationale for firms to adopt these performance-enhancing practices, and public policy can play a valuable role in spreading this information. Furthermore, there is a very strong case to be made for supportive public policy of employee ownership if employee ownership firms lay off fewer workers and are more likely to survive, since the economic and social costs of layoffs and firm failures are borne by workers, families, communities, and the larger economy and society. In economic terms, the layoffs and firm failures create negative externalities that can justify the use of supportive public policies. In addition, a policy case can be built on the third source of interest listed above—increasing broad-based prosperity, which can reduce inequality and strengthen democracy. We discuss the policy implications further in the concluding chapter, taking all of these arguments into account.

There are nonetheless concerns about employee ownership that may limit the interest of companies and policymakers. The two principal concerns are these:

1) **The free rider problem.** The individual incentive to be a "free rider" in group incentives grows with the size of the group. This is also often called the "$1/N$ problem," since in a group incentive plan with N workers the average worker will receive only $1/N$ of the extra rewards generated by his or her individual effort. This may be counteracted by workplace norms and company policies to encourage cooperation, higher effort, and monitoring of fellow workers, as will be discussed.

2) **Financial risk.** Stock values can obviously go up and down, and having a large share of one's wealth in any one asset— including the stock of one's employer—means that one may face financial risk by not being appropriately diversified. The financial risk may be increased under employee ownership, since if the firm fails the employee can lose both his or her job

and the company stock value. While this is an important concern and deserves attention in policy, we will review theoretical and empirical evidence that it does not appear to be a major problem in practice.

PLAN OF THE BOOK

This book presents new evidence focused on the second major source of interest listed above: the stability and survival of employee-ownership firms. These topics are the most relevant to discussions of public policy support for employee ownership, given the potential broader benefits for the economy and society. In the remainder of this chapter, we provide an overview of the major types of employee ownership and prior evidence relevant to each of the four sources of interest and the two main objections. Following a brief history and overview of the prevalence of employee ownership in Chapter 2, we present new data on the relationship of employee ownership to employment stability in Chapter 3, and of employee ownership to firm survival in Chapter 4. We further probe these results in Chapter 5 in order to understand the role of compensation flexibility and higher productivity as potential explanations for the greater stability and survival of employee ownership firms. Apart from helping us interpret the stability and survival results, the evidence in Chapter 5 also sheds light on the first source of interest identified above—improving economic performance—by analyzing the relationship of employee ownership to productivity, and it sheds light on the financial risk objection by assessing pay levels and flexibility in employee ownership companies. Chapter 6 concludes with a summary of our key results and their implications for public policy.

WHAT IS MEANT BY "EMPLOYEE OWNERSHIP"?

There is great variety in the types and extent of employee ownership. The extent of employee ownership within a firm can vary along three dimensions: 1) the percentage of the company owned by employees (from a minority stake to 100 percent ownership), 2) the percentage of employees who participate in ownership (from a minority to 100 percent), and 3) the distribution of shares among employee owners (from perfect equality to a very unequal distribution where one manager owns the majority of stock and each of the other employees owns only a small amount). Regarding Dimension 1, in this study we measure the percentage of publicly held companies owned by broad-based plans, so that we can examine the effects of the percentage of company owned. Because they are publicly held companies, none are 100 percent employee owned, and most have only a small percentage owned by employees. Regarding Dimensions 2 and 3, we include only broad-based employee ownership as defined by pension rules governing coverage, so that all or most employees will be included and the distribution of ownership will generally be proportional to pay and tenure.

Overall, an estimated 22.9 million employees, or almost one-fifth of U.S. private sector employees, own stock in the companies they work for (the prevalence will be explored more fully in Chapter 2). Employee ownership programs can take several different forms, summarized in Table 1.1.

- One of the most prevalent forms of employee ownership in the United States is the ESOP. In an ESOP, ERISA allows companies to contribute company stock, or money to buy stock, to an

Table 1.1 Population Covered by Various Employee Ownership Plans

Types of employee ownership	Number of employees covered in U.S.
ESOPs	10.6 million
401(k) plans	5.7 million
Other pension plans	184,000
Employee stock purchase plans	Unknown
Worker cooperatives	About 7,500
Individual purchases on open market	Unknown
Stock held after exercising stock options	8.5 million stock option holders, though the number holding stock after exercising their option is unknown
Any employee ownership	22.9 million

SOURCE: Authors' compilation.

employee pension trust, or to borrow money to fund employee ownership and then repay it in installments from company revenues. Under this approach, workers generally gain an ownership stake without investing their own money to buy the stock (although in a small minority of cases they have taken wage or benefit concessions to fund the stock purchase) (Blasi and Kruse 1991). As of 2012, there were 10.6 million employee participants in ESOPs (USDOL 2015).

Apart from ESOPs, employee ownership may occur through the following ways:

- In 401(k) retirement pension plans, companies may match pretax employee contributions with company stock, and employees may choose to invest some of their own contributions in company stock. As of 2012, there were 5.7 million employee participants in non-ESOP 401(k) plans with employer stock (Table 2.2 in Chapter 2).

- In other pension plans, such as deferred profit-sharing plans without a 401(k) option, the company invests a portion of the profit-sharing contribution into company stock. These are rare: in 2012, there were only 184,000 participants in non-ESOP, non-401(k) pension plans with employer stock (Table 2.2 in Chapter 2).

- Employee stock purchase plans (ESPPs) typically offer stock at a 10 to 15 percent discount to the stock market price so that employees can acquire ownership through individual decisions to purchase company stock. About half of all large companies in the United States offer ESPPs, and an average of 30 percent of employees in these companies participate in the ESPP (Babenko and Sen 2014).

- Worker cooperatives are 100 percent—or nearly 100 percent—worker-owned companies in which workers invest in ownership stakes and typically make decisions based on one-person/one-vote, rather than having voting rights based on number of shares of stock. These are much less common than other forms of employee ownership; an attempted census of U.S. cooperatives found that they had a total of only about 7,500 employees in 2009 (Deller et al. 2009), although they are more common in several other countries.

- Employees can make individual purchases of company stock on the open market.
- Employees can exercise their stock options. Stock options give them the right to buy company stock at a preset strike price after a specific vesting period. Once the vesting period is over, the worker has the choice to exercise the stock option—i.e., to exercise his or her right to buy the stock at the preset strike price and sell at the going market stock price. The worker will have an incentive to exercise the stock option when the market price is above the strike price and thereby obtain a positive payoff. In this way, the employee gets the upside gain of a rise in share price without the downside risk of losing part of his or her investment. An important point is that stock-option holdings only constitute employee ownership if and when they are exercised, which would only occur when the stock price goes above the strike price and the exerciser exercises the option but continues to hold the stock. Thus, stock options could lead to employee ownership, but they do not strictly constitute employee ownership in and of themselves. Therefore, when we present descriptive statistics or figures on stock options in this book, we will always treat stock options separately rather than including them in our statistics or figures on employee ownership. Unlike direct purchases of company stock, stock options are not purchased with employee savings unless they are used for wage substitution. While stock options are most common in executive compensation, a number of companies—particularly high-tech companies—have implemented broad-based plans that distribute stock options to all or most employees. As of 2014, there were about 8.5 million employees holding stock options (Table 2.1 in Chapter 2).

WHAT DOES THE EVIDENCE SHOW?

Previous empirical research has shown employee ownership to be linked to a multitude of improved outcomes. There are several alternative methods that have been used in this research:

- Compare employee owners to individuals who are not employee owners.

- Compare outcomes at firms that have employee ownership to otherwise comparable firms that do not have such programs.

- Follow firms longitudinally and compare them before and after adoption of employee ownership relative to firms that did not adopt employee ownership.

- Employ laboratory or field experiments to examine the link between financial participation and performance outcomes.

On the following pages is an overview of prior evidence for each of the four major sources of interest—1) increased economic performance, 2) greater job security and firm survival, 3) shared prosperity, and 4) lower labor-management conflict and higher quality of work life—and for the two major objections (free riding and financial risk). We start each section with some results from the General Social Survey (GSS), which illustrate the basic relationship between employee ownership and outcomes of interest, and then provide more detail on the in-depth scholarly research. The GSS is a nationally representative survey conducted by the National Opinion Research Center at the University of Chicago. The GSS is conducted every two years on approximately 1,500 adults and includes questions on a wide variety of topics on social, demographic, and economic factors, such as political and civic participation, life satisfaction, and work habits. The GSS included several questions on employee ownership, stock options, and profit sharing in 2002, 2006, 2010, and 2014, which are useful in illustrating the trends and potential effects of these pay systems.[1]

Economic performance. The GSS results in Figure 1.1 are consistent with the popular view that employees tend to work harder and raise productivity under employee ownership. Survey respondents were asked how hard they thought their coworkers worked. Respondents who were employee owners reported that their coworkers had higher average effort (on a 0–10 scale) than was reported by employee non-owners. It is important to note that this question does not reveal whether the other workers at the respondent's workplace also participate in employee ownership; however, employee ownership programs tend to

Figure 1.1 Workplace Effort and Employee Ownership

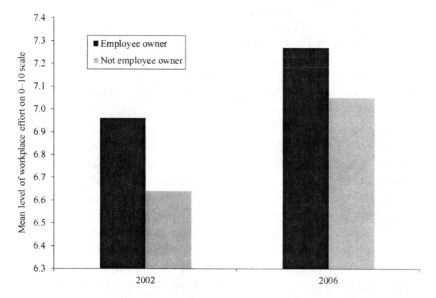

NOTE: Data are based on responses to the General Social Survey (GSS) variable *cowrkhrd*, which asks, "At your workplace, how hard would you say that people work, with 0 meaning not at all hard and 10 meaning very hard?" (The GSS asked this question only in 2002 and 2006.) This figure illustrates mean response by employee ownership.
SOURCE: Data are from the GSS on employees at private firms.

be implemented at the workplace level, so it is likely that most of an employee-owner respondent's coworkers are also employee owners.

The results of this simple comparison are consistent with prior studies that demonstrate a positive association between employee ownership and company performance. Two reviews of the employee ownership literature have concluded that "two-thirds of 129 studies (including both performance and attitude studies) on employee ownership and its consequences found favorable effects relating to employee ownership, while one-tenth found negative effects" (Kaarsemaker 2006) and "research on ESOPs and employee ownership is overwhelmingly positive and largely credible" (Freeman 2007). Formal meta-analyses that statistically test the combined results of studies have found strong evidence of a positive association between employee ownership and performance (Doucouliagos 1995; Kruse and Blasi 1997; O'Boyle, Patel, and Gonzalez-Mulé, forthcoming).

Examples of individual studies include one sponsored by the United Kingdom Treasury (Oxera Consulting 2007a,b,c) that aimed to understand whether government policies that encouraged firms to introduce employee ownership improved firm performance. The study obtained data from confidential tax records, and its examination of tax-advantaged share schemes at more than 16,000 UK firms reveals that broad-based employee ownership improves firm performance measures such as value-added and turnover. A parallel study using publicly available data on British corporations with broad-based employee ownership finds similar results. It also finds that the effects were greatly influenced by the delegation of decision-making autonomy from management to employees (Bryson and Freeman 2010). Also, Jones and Kato (1995) examine the effect of broad-based employee stock ownership plans by estimating production functions using a panel of Japanese firms; they find that the introduction of an ESOP resulted in a 4–5 percent increase in productivity and that this productivity payoff took from three to four years to actualize. In the United States, a study by Blasi, Freeman, and Kruse (2013) examined 300 privately held firms that set up ESOPs between 1988 and 1994, comparing each ESOP firm to a similar company of the same size and in the same industry without an ESOP. This study finds that ESOP firms have significantly higher sales growth and higher sales per worker than matching firms without ESOPs.

Of course, correlation does not imply causation. For example, companies may have good performance even before adopting employee ownership, so that good performance is a cause rather than consequence of employee ownership. To address this possibility, many studies have used longitudinal data that compare performance before and after the adoption of a plan, or that examine other variation in employee ownership over time (e.g., in percentage covered or size of stakes), and have found that performance improves after employee ownership is adopted or expanded. While these studies control for anything special about the firm that does not change over time, there may be other factors that affect the firm's choice of *when* to adopt a participatory pay plan, and that may be responsible for any performance changes. To address this possibility, many of the studies on this topic have used special methods to adjust for any statistical bias, and these studies have continued to find generally positive results.[2]

Another potentially confounding factor is that higher-quality workers may be more likely to join participatory pay firms, and the higher firm performance may be due to the presence of better workers rather than the direct effect of employee ownership. If employee ownership does attract better workers, this could be a good reason for an individual firm to adopt employee ownership, but it does not provide a strong case for policy support, since any expansion of employee ownership may be essentially reshuffling workers among firms and not raising overall performance of the economy. While this issue of worker self-selection has not been examined in the context of employee ownership, there have been two studies of other group incentives that have found that average worker quality does not change as compensation is changed from individual to group incentives, whereas average worker performance improves under the group incentives (Hansen 1997; Weiss 1987).

The interpretation that employee ownership increases productivity on average is supported by findings on employees' performance-related behaviors. A study of over 40,000 workers finds that those who owned company stock are more likely to say they would take action if they saw a fellow worker not working well, by talking to the worker, a supervisor, or members of the work team (Freeman, Kruse, and Blasi 2010). This result occurred both before and after controlling for a wide variety of job and personal characteristics. The idea that shared rewards is a causal factor was strongly supported in employee reports of why they would take such actions (e.g., "Poor performance will cost me and other employees in bonus or stock value"). Employee owners also reported lower levels of turnover, more pride and loyalty to the company, greater willingness to work hard to help the company, and more suggestions to improve performance (Blasi et al. 2010). While this study does not find lower absenteeism among employee owners, a French study finds that employee ownership plans were linked to reductions in employee absenteeism (Brown, Fakhfakh, and Sessions 1999).

All the studies described above are based on field research on actual firms and workers participating in employee ownership. While these studies control for many observable factors, it is always possible that there are some unobserved factors affecting the results. These unobserved factors can be fully ruled out only in a true experiment with random assignment. While random assignment of employee owner-ship in actual work settings would be extremely difficult to implement, laboratory experiments have found higher productivity among subjects randomly assigned to be in employee-owned "firms" (Frohlich et al. 1998; Mellizo 2013), suggesting that there can be true causal effects of employee ownership on performance.

Job Security and Firm Survival. The GSS results show that both actual layoffs (Figure 1.2) and the perceived likelihood of layoff (Figure 1.3) are lower for employee-owners than for nonowners. As we can see in Figure 1.2, in each year, workers who participated in employee own-ership programs indicated a lower incidence of losing their jobs than workers who were not employee owners. For example, in 2002, 3.0 percent of employee owners reported being laid off from their jobs in the past year compared to 9.2 percent of non–employee owners. In each

Figure 1.2 Layoffs and Employee Ownership

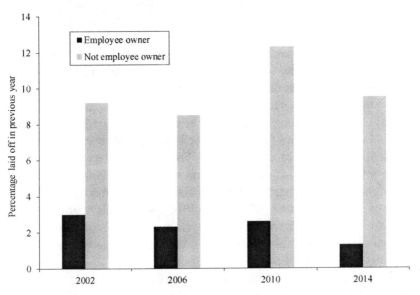

NOTE: Layoff information based on the GSS variable *laidoff*, which indicates whether the employee was laid off from his or her main job at any time in the past year. Figure illustrates mean response by employee ownership.
SOURCE: Data are from the GSS on employees at private firms.

Figure 1.3 Perceived Likelihood of Layoff and Employee Ownership

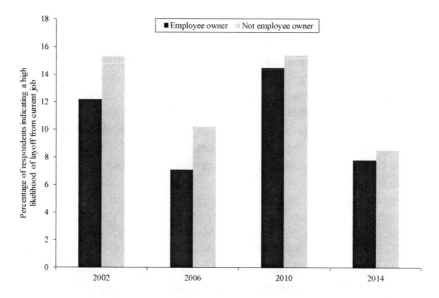

NOTE: Layoff information based on the GSS variable *joblose*, which asks the respondent how likely he/she is to lose his/her job in the coming year. Responses "very likely" and "fairly likely" were coded as high layoff likelihood, while responses "not too likely" and "not at all likely" were coded as low layoff likelihood. Figure illustrates mean response by employee ownership.
SOURCE: Data are from the GSS on employees at private firms.

year, employee ownership participants also reported a lower likelihood of losing their jobs than workers who were not employee owners, as seen in Figure 1.3. For example, in 2002, 12.2 percent of GSS respondents who were employee owners indicated a high layoff likelihood in the coming year (either "very likely" or "fairly likely"), while 15.3 percent of non–employee owners reported a high layoff likelihood. The difference in actual layoffs is particularly strong in the Great Recession year of 2010, when 12.3 percent of nonowners reported being laid off in the past year compared to only 2.6 percent of employee owners. One potential criticism of the layoff comparisons is that this difference may reflect the greater average job tenure of employee owners, since the nonowners may be new employees who are more likely to be laid off in recessions. The results are maintained, however, when restricted to employees with more than one year of tenure, and when controlling for tenure, occupation, gender, race, age, and education.

Employee ownership may be linked to lower layoffs because of enhanced company employment stability and survival. Employee ownership may lead to this in at least four related ways, including 1) increasing productivity through greater cooperation, information sharing, and commitment (Pierce, Rubenfeld, and Morgan 1991); 2) reducing dysfunctional workplace conflict that can contribute to firm failure; 3) increasing employee investments in valuable firm-specific skills; and 4) creating a workplace culture that instills a sense of psychological ownership, with a corresponding commitment to preserve employee jobs whenever possible.

Prior evidence from U.S. studies shows that firms with employee ownership have higher survival rates: public companies with substantial employee ownership stakes in 1983 were 20 percent more likely than closely matched industry pairs to survive through 1995 (Blair, Kruse, and Blasi 2002), and those with substantial employee ownership stakes in 1988 were 21 percent more likely to survive through 2001 (Park, Kruse, and Sesil 2004). A study that focused on closely held firms used a similar methodology of matching ESOP and non-ESOP companies in the same industry and found that ESOP companies in 1988 were only half as likely as non-ESOP firms to go bankrupt or close over the 1988–1999 period, and only three-fifths as likely to disappear for any reason (Blasi, Freeman, and Kruse 2013). These three studies also found greater employment stability among the employee ownership firms compared to their same-industry pairs, as measured by the standard deviation of the logarithm of employment. Also, Welbourne and Cyr (1999) found that among companies with initial public offerings in 1988, those with broad-based employee ownership had higher survival rates. A study of S corporations with ESOPs over the 2006–2011 period found that they had higher average employment growth in the 2006–2008 prerecession period than did the economy as a whole, and they also had faster growth following the recession from 2009 to 2011 (Brill 2012, p. 6).

The greater stability of employee ownership firms is linked to substantially lower government costs for unemployment compensation and forgone tax revenues. An analysis based on the GSS results in combination with government data on unemployment compensation and tax rates concludes that "based on the estimated cost of each unemployed worker, the implied federal savings from the lower layoff rates for employee owners is $23.3 billion for the recession year 2010 and $13.7 billion per year for the longer 2002–2010 period" (Employee Ownership Foundation 2013; Rosen 2013).

Apart from these U.S. results on stability and survival, there have been four studies of worker cooperatives outside the United States that have found high survival rates compared to conventional firms. These were studies of worker cooperatives in several countries by Ben-Ner (1988), in the United Kingdom by Thomas and Cornforth (1989), in France by Pérotin (2004), and in Uruguay by Burdín (2014). The last of these studies analyzed a long panel of administrative firm-level data maintained by the government and found that worker cooperatives had a 29 percent lower rate of dissolution than did conventional firms, and that the higher survival rate is associated with greater employment stability.

More-broadly shared prosperity. Employee ownership will not enhance worker incomes if it substitutes for standard worker pay or benefits. In this case it presents serious issues of financial risk, since variable pay is being substituted for fixed pay (although financial risk may nonetheless be reduced by greater job security, as will be discussed). While a common perception is that employee ownership will substitute for other forms of compensation, the evidence indicates that employee ownership tends to come on top of market levels of pay. The GSS data in Figure 1.4 provide a simple comparison to illustrate this point. Employee-owners are slightly more likely than non–employee owners to report that their fixed pay levels are at or above market levels, meaning that the employee ownership comes on top of market levels of fixed pay for most workers.

There are some cases in which employee ownership is used as part of wage or benefit concessions, but these are rare (despite the media attention paid to several cases).[3] A comprehensive longitudinal study of all ESOP adoptions over the period 1980–2001 finds that employee wages (excluding ESOP contributions) either increased (for small ESOPs) or stayed constant (for large ESOPs) after adoption, controlling for state-level and industry-level wage changes and other company characteristics (Kim and Ouimet 2014). Consistent with this, cross-

Figure 1.4 Employee Ownership and Fixed Pay Relative to Market

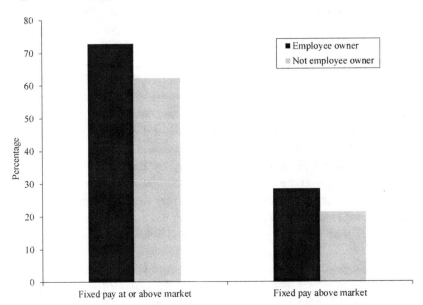

NOTE: Data are based on the GSS variable *compwage*, which asks "Do you believe your fixed annual wages last year were higher or lower than those of employees with similar experience and job descriptions in other companies in your region? Please answer on a 1-to-5 scale." Responses of "4" or "5" were classified as "fixed pay above market," and answers of "3" or more were classified as "fixed pay at or above market." Figure illustrates mean response by employee ownership.
SOURCE: Data are from the 2014 wave of the GSS on employees at private firms.

sectional comparisons of matched ESOP and non-ESOP firms have found similar levels of pay and other benefits in the two types of firms, so that ESOPs appear to come on top of other worker pay and benefits (Kardas, Scharf, and Keogh 1998; Scharf and Mackin 2000).

Apart from ESOPs, employee ownership in general is linked to higher overall pay. More detailed analysis of the GSS data, with controls for job and demographic characteristics, finds that employee owners have higher levels of yearly earnings and are more likely to say they are "paid what they deserve" and that their fringe benefits are good (Kruse, Freeman, and Blasi 2010, p. 266). Other cross-sectional studies find that employee ownership is associated with higher average compensation levels (Blasi, Conte, and Kruse 1996), pension assets (Kroumova 2000), and overall worker wealth (Buchele et al. 2010).

For example, a study of more than 40,000 workers finds that an extra dollar of employee ownership value is associated with an extra 94 cents of wealth, indicating that there is very little substitution between employee ownership and other forms of wealth; thus, employee-owned stock appears to add to wealth in general (Buchele et al. 2010). While some of these forms of employee ownership involve workers directly purchasing stock (such as in Employee Stock Purchase Plans), such purchases are generally done on favorable terms for the employees (e.g., with discounts). The clear evidence that ESOP participants receive stock on top of regular compensation, and that employee owners in general receive higher pay, indicates that employee ownership generally does not substitute for regular fixed pay.

How can this be? How is it possible that employee ownership can simply add to, rather than substitute for, other forms of pay or wealth? One interpretation that integrates the accumulated evidence about worker behavior, productivity, and pay levels is based on theories of reciprocity and gift exchange. The idea that reciprocity is important in economic and social relationships receives strong support from laboratory and field studies (Axelrod 1984; Fehr and Gächter 2000; Gintis et al. 2005). This idea has been formalized in the efficiency wage model of "gift exchange," in which workers respond to the "gift" of above-market compensation with a reciprocal "gift" of high effort and cooperation to benefit the firm and fellow workers (Akerlof 1982). There has been substantial empirical evidence in support of efficiency wage models of the labor market (as shown by the meta-analysis in Peach and Stanley [2009]). Giving employees the opportunity to own stock on top of regular compensation may be an especially effective "gift" for creating and reinforcing a sense of common purpose and encouraging higher commitment and productivity (Blasi et al. 2010). This is consistent with the studies finding higher average productivity under employee ownership, summarized above. Recent evidence lends further support to this interpretation, finding that positive effects of employee ownership on attitudes and behaviors are much more likely to occur when employee ownership comes on top of market-level wages and benefits (Weltmann, Blasi, and Kruse 2015).

The consistent finding that employee ownership tends to be "gravy" on top of other pay and wealth means that it may be a promising means for increasing worker incomes and wealth in general, which may help to reduce inequality. A 1986 General Accounting Office (GAO) report concludes that "the distribution of stock ownership within ESOPs appears to be broader than is the case in the population at large," but that there were too few ESOP participants for this to make a noticeable difference in the overall distribution of stock ownership or wealth in general during this time—a time when ESOPs had just begun (USGAO 1986, p. 43). The first GAO conclusion is supported by more recent data, which finds that the distribution of wealth among employees in employee ownership companies is more equal than among all employees or households in general (Buchele et al. 2010). These results suggest that expansion of employee ownership has potential for enhancing the broad-based sharing of economic prosperity.

Lower labor-management conflict and higher quality of work life. Employee ownership may help to create a harmonious workplace, with workers having a greater say in decisions and other improvements in their workplace experiences.

Does employee ownership in fact create more harmonious workplaces? One study found that strikes were less common in unionized companies that adopted ESOPs (Cramton, Mehran, and Tracy 2008), which may reflect the greater financial transparency of unionized ESOP companies (Bova, Dou, and Hope 2015). Employees tend to give companies higher ratings on management-employee relations and other aspects of company treatment of employees (e.g., handling of promotions, worker safety, and trustworthiness) when they are employee owners or otherwise participate in shared rewards (Kruse, Freeman, and Blasi 2010).

Two basic measures of the quality of work life are workers' turnover intentions and workers' job satisfaction. The GSS data in Figure 1.5 show the relationship between workers' turnover intentions and ownership. In each year, workers with employee ownership indicated a lower level of intention to find a new job than workers who did not participate in employee ownership; for example, in 2002, nearly 23 percent of nonemployee owners indicated a high likelihood of turnover intention, compared to 13 percent of employee owners. This difference

Figure 1.5 Turnover Intention and Employee Ownership

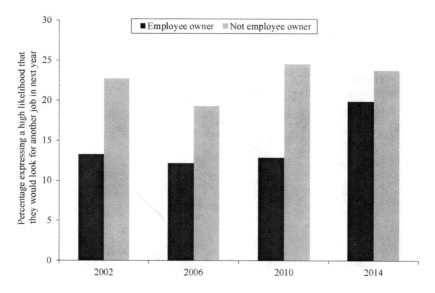

NOTE: Turnover intention information is based on the GSS variable *trynewjb*, which asks the respondent how likely he or she is to make a genuine effort to find a new job with another employer within the coming year. The response "very likely" was coded as high turnover intention, while responses "somewhat likely" and "not at all likely" were coded as low turnover intention. Figure illustrates mean response by employee ownership.
SOURCE: Data are from the GSS on employees at private firms.

is maintained over time, although the gap narrows in 2014. A more detailed analysis of the turnover data shows that employees who are owners are less likely than other employees to say they will look for a new job, after controlling for detailed job and personal characteristics (Blasi et al. 2010). In addition, a recent analysis of the "Great Place to Work" data set—which includes more than 700 firms and 230,000 workers—shows that worker intent to stay with the company is significantly higher in ESOP companies than in non-ESOP companies (Blasi, Freeman, and Kruse 2016).

The relation of employee ownership to the other basic measure of the quality of work life—job satisfaction—is illustrated in Figure 1.6. This shows that employee ownership and job satisfaction are positively

Figure 1.6 Job Satisfaction and Employee Ownership

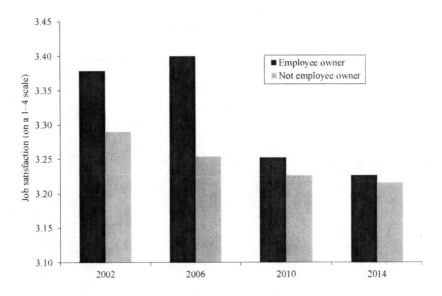

NOTE: Data are based on the GSS variable *satjob1*, which asks how satisfied employees are with their jobs on a scale of 1 ("not at all") to 4 ("very"). The figure illustrates
mean job satisfaction by year.
SOURCE: Data are from the GSS on employees at private firms.

related in the 2002, 2006, 2010, and 2014 waves of the GSS. The difference between employee owners and non–employee owners is very
small, however, in 2010 and 2014, which could reflect low stock values
and uncertainty following the Great Recession.

Further probing of the job satisfaction and turnover intention results
shows that any favorable effects of employee ownership appear to be
very dependent on the presence of other supportive workplace policies.
An index combining employee ownership and stock options with other
shared rewards (profit sharing and gainsharing) was found to predict
higher job satisfaction and lower turnover intentions only when combined with high-performance work policies (employee involvement,
training, and job security) and low levels of supervision; without such
policies, the effect on job satisfaction was in fact negative (Blasi et al.
2010; Kruse, Freeman, and Blasi 2010).

This latter result may reflect mixed messages to employees when they are given employee ownership or stock options without supportive workplace policies: "We want you to be more productive as employee-owners, but we're not going to give you the tools to be more productive, and we're going to keep a close eye on you" (Kruse, Freeman, and Blasi 2010, pp. 274–275). In such cases, employee ownership may be seen primarily as an attempt to shift financial risk onto workers, rather than to empower workers.

Therefore, an important question is whether employee ownership is generally accompanied by supportive workplace policies. The GSS data show that employee financial participation goes hand in hand with workplace practices that empower workers with the ability to improve workplace performance (and thereby increase their payoff from having a share in company ownership), particularly employee involvement in decision making and firm-sponsored employee training. One of the 2006 GSS survey questions asks the following: "Some companies have organized workplace decision-making in ways to get more employee input and involvement. Are you personally involved in any group, team, committee, or task force that addresses issues such as product quality, cost cutting, productivity, health and safety, or another workplace issue?" Forty-three percent of employee owners responded affirmatively to this question in 2006, and 34 percent did so in 2014, compared to only 28 percent and 29 percent in those two years among nonowners, as seen in Figure 1.7. A similar relationship exists with respect to firm-sponsored employee training. As seen in Figure 1.8, nearly 65 percent of employee owners in 2006 reported that they had received formal training from their current employers in the past year, and 69 percent did so in 2014, compared to only 44 percent and 42 percent of nonowners in those two years. These relationships are strongly maintained when controlling for other job and personal characteristics (Bryson and Freeman 2010; Dube and Freeman 2010; Kruse, Freeman, and Blasi 2010).

The higher prevalence of participation in decision making and training among employee owners suggests that there are complementarities of these policies with financial participation. Most basically, this points to the importance of providing employee owners with the *means* to improve performance—through increased skills and opportunities for input—so that they can effectively take action in response to the financial incentives. In the language of economics, "residual control"

Figure 1.7 Employee Involvement in Decision Making and Employee Ownership

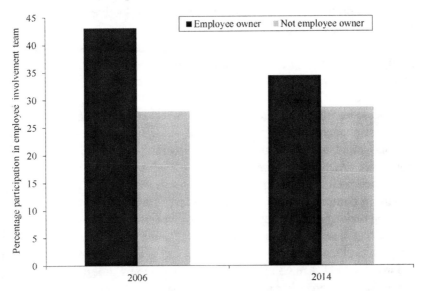

NOTE: Data are based on the GSS variable *empinput*, which asks, "Some companies have organized workplace decision-making in ways to get more employee input and involvement. Are you personally involved in any group, team, committee, or task force that addresses issues such as product quality, cost cutting, productivity, health and safety, or another workplace issue?" The figure illustrates the share of employees who responded affirmatively to this question.
SOURCE: Data are from the GSS on employees at private firms.

should be combined with "residual returns" in order to provide proper incentives. As noted earlier, prior evidence has supported the idea that employee involvement, training, and job security combine with shared rewards in improving performance-related attitudes and behaviors.

In summary of the literature on labor-management conflict and quality of work life, the above results—plus other studies reviewed in Kruse, Freeman, and Blasi (2010)—indicate that employee ownership is linked to the following results:

- fewer strikes and better evaluations of workplace relations
- lower turnover and higher job satisfaction, but only when shared rewards are combined with high-performance policies

Figure 1.8 Employer-Sponsored Training and Employee Ownership

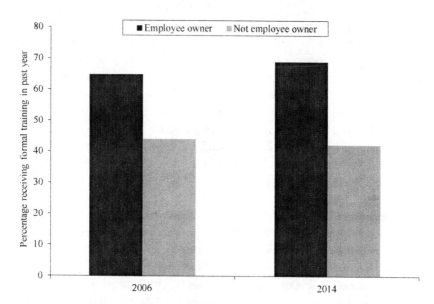

NOTE: Data are based on the GSS variable *emptrain*, which asks, "In the last 12 months, have you received any formal training from your current employer, such as in classes or seminars sponsored by the employer?" The figure illustrates the share of employees who responded affirmatively to this question.
SOURCE: Data are from the GSS on employees at private firms.

- greater employee participation in decisions
- higher likelihood of company-sponsored training
- higher levels of pay
- higher job security

Free rider problem. Group incentives can clearly dilute the individual incentive to work hard, and thereby they can hamper productivity gains from share plans. However, as discussed above in the review of evidence on economic performance, it does not appear to prevent employee ownership firms from having higher productivity on average. Game theory shows that the free rider problem (an example of the "prisoner's dilemma") can be overcome in a cooperative equilibrium in which everyone can agree on and enforce high work norms (Axelrod 1984; Fudenberg and Maskin 1986). Such cooperation may be created and maintained by policies that build team spirit, loyalty, and peer pressure to perform well. This idea is supported by the finding that positive effects of group incentives on attitudes and behaviors are more likely to occur when employees are covered by high-performance work policies (employee involvement, training, and job security) and are given freedom to work without close supervision (Blasi et al. 2010). In addition, the finding that employee owners are more likely than nonowners to take action against shirking coworkers indicates that the free rider problem is often overcome by worker comonitoring and enforcement of higher norms.

Financial risk. The financial risk that can result from tying worker pay and wealth to firm performance is an important concern. A fundamental premise of portfolio theory is that portfolios should be structured to balance risk and reward, and that diversification is important to mitigate risk. Having a large portion of one's wealth portfolio in any one asset means that the portfolio may not be properly diversified, and a plunge in the value of that asset can cause a significant decline in the portfolio's overall value. The financial risk may be greater with employer stock than with other assets, since if the company does poorly the worker could lose his or her job along with a decline in wealth, possibly endangering his or her retirement security.

It is undoubtedly true that some workers have too much of their wealth tied up in a single asset and thus are not properly diversified. For example, each year many people use some or all of their life savings to start their own businesses. As with entrepreneurs who are heavily invested in their businesses, employee ownership may sometimes contribute to improper diversification. The financial risk from employee ownership, however, does not appear to be a major problem in practice, as indicated by the following research findings:

Employee ownership generally comes on top of standard pay and benefits. It is important to reemphasize that workers do not pay for stock with their wages or savings in ESOPs, the most prevalent form of employee ownership in the United States. As noted above in the discussion of broad-based prosperity, there is strong evidence that most employee owners receive fixed pay and benefits that are at or above market level, and that firms do not lower base pay as they adopt ESOPs except in rare situations, when they may make a concession. Employer stock generally adds to, rather than substitutes for, other forms of wealth. This greatly mitigates any financial risk, since workers are not sacrificing for risky pay—the employee ownership may be seen as "gravy" on top of regular pay, which appears to be crucial in improving employees' performance-related attitudes and behaviors, as discussed above.

Increased job security reduces financial risk. The biggest form of financial risk faced by most workers is job loss, as opposed to market fluctuations in the value of their financial assets. If employee ownership does contribute to employment stability and firm survival, as suggested by past studies and as explored in this book, employee owners may face less financial risk than other employees.

Even risk-averse employees tend to like these plans. One surprising finding from the NBER study of more than 40,000 employees is that two-thirds of the most risk-averse employees reported that they would like at least some ownership, profit sharing, or stock options in their pay package. For example, among those who rated themselves as 3 or lower on a 0–10 scale of how much they like to take risks (with 0 = "hating to take any kind of risk" and 10 = "loving to take risks"), 66 percent said they would prefer to be paid at least in part with profit sharing, stock, or stock options as opposed to entirely with a fixed wage or salary. Also, 55 percent of this group wanted their next pay increase to be split between fixed wages and profit sharing, stock, or options, and 12 percent wanted it all to be in the form of profit sharing, stock, or options (Kruse, Blasi, and Park 2010). Risk aversion clearly influences attitudes toward variable pay, since the above figures were even higher among those who are less risk averse, but these results indicate that even risk-averse employees are open to employee ownership and other variable pay plans.

Along with these empirical findings, researchers find the following:

Recent theory shows that employee ownership can be part of an efficient diversified portfolio. Harry Markowitz, who won the Nobel Prize in economics for portfolio theory, explicitly rejects the idea that risk aversion precludes employee ownership. His theory concludes that substantial amounts of a single asset—including stock in one's company—can be part of an efficient portfolio as long as the overall portfolio is properly diversified (Markowitz, Blasi, and Kruse 2010).

In sum, employee ownership has been seen as relevant to economic performance, job security, macroeconomic stability, and economic inequality, with potential implications for firms, workers, the economy, and society as a whole. Prior studies provide evidence that it is often associated with better outcomes for firms and workers, and that the free rider and risk problems are important but may be overcome under the right circumstances. There is very little evidence, however, on how employee ownership relates to employment stability and firm survival, which is the focus of this book. We will spend the latter half of this book presenting new evidence on the link between employee ownership and employment stability and firm survival. However, before presenting our findings, it will be helpful to set the stage by first reviewing the history and current prevalence of employee ownership, which we turn to now in Chapter 2.

Notes

1. The Employee Ownership Foundation provided significant funding for the collection of data from the employee ownership module of the GSS.
2. These methods include instrumental variables, two-stage least squares, and Heckman corrections.
3. In one study, only 4 percent of ESOPs were adopted as part of wage and benefit concessions (USGAO 1986). Of the nearly 1,000 public companies that developed sizable employee ownership stakes in the 1980s, there were only 26 cases of trading stock for wages and 41 cases of terminating defined benefit plans (Blasi and Kruse 1991, pp. 325–328).

2
Prevalence of Employee Ownership

This chapter sets the stage for the new evidence presented in the forthcoming chapters by providing background on the history and prevalence of employee ownership. In this chapter, we first review the historical roots of employee ownership in the United States. Employee ownership as we know it today takes various forms, as discussed in Chapter 1, such as Employee Stock Ownership Plans (ESOPs) and stock ownership in 401(k) pension plans. However, these tools are relatively recent manifestations of the notion of broad-based sharing of company revenue with employees. The earliest manifestations of the idea of workers having an ownership stake in the firms where they work came during the era of the American Revolution, in the closely related notion of profit sharing.[1] Therefore, a discussion of the historical roots of employee ownership in the United States necessarily involves the discussion of early implementation of profit sharing. We review the early history of profit sharing as envisioned by the founding fathers of the United States and implemented during that time, followed by its implementation by firms during the era of industrialization. We then go on to review more recent prevalence of employee ownership using evidence from large data sets—namely, the General Social Survey and the U.S. Department of Labor Form 5500 files. We also present evidence on how the prevalence of employee ownership varies by firm industry, firm size, and worker occupation. Finally, we discuss the prevalence of employee ownership in countries other than the United States.

HISTORICAL ROOTS OF EMPLOYEE OWNERSHIP IN THE UNITED STATES

Cod Fisheries and Whaling in New England

The idea of workers having an ownership stake in the firms where they work has a long and rich history in the United States, and its roots can be traced all the way back to the philosophies of the founding fathers of the republic.

Cod fishing and whaling were among the most important industries in New England during the early years of the nation. Throughout the 1700s, seamen on cod and whaling ships very commonly had a stake in the overall profit their ship made. Crews shared the rewards of successful hauls, including the lowest-level members of the crew, and were called "sharesmen." Some fishermen even had ownership shares in the ship, which made them investors in the business as well as recipients of the profit shares as workers.

George Washington's Treasury secretary, Alexander Hamilton, was a proponent of such share schemes and advanced a bill that strengthened this practice, which Congress passed in 1792 and President Washington signed into law. The U.S. government wanted to rebuild the cod fishing fleet, which had essentially served as the navy and was decimated by the British in the Revolutionary War. Building on the sharing tradition in the industry, the law mandated tax credits to cod fisheries, which would be divided among the vessel's owners and the crew (three-eighths to the owners and five-eighths to the crew), and the credit would be granted only if the shipowner had a written contract before the voyage that stipulated that the profit from the entire catch would be shared with all the sailors. The shipowner could collect the credit only if he could produce this agreement. The law stayed in force for many years. In 1803, President Jefferson's secretary of the Treasury, Albert Gallatin, reported to the Speaker of the House of Representatives on how the legislation had helped to strengthen the cod fishing industry. Gallatin was a strong proponent of broad-based sharing, elsewhere saying that "the democratic principle upon which this Nation was founded should not be restricted to the political processes but should be applied to the industrial operation" (U.S. Senate 1939, p. 72). The cod fishery law continued well into the nineteenth century. The federal government's requirement that the cod fishery tax subsidy law be shared among the crew is the first documented case in American history where the government made citizen shares a condition for receiving a tax break (Blasi, Freeman, and Kruse 2013).

Broad-Based Sharing in the 1800s and Early 1900s

During the late 1800s, the nation's leading industrialists, such as Charles Pillsbury, Andrew Carnegie, and John D. Rockefeller, embraced the notion of employee ownership and profit sharing and actively implemented broad-based shared capitalism programs in their companies.[2] Many of these companies succeeded in meeting the market test of surviving in a competitive economy and are still successful to this day. In 1882, Charles Pillsbury, whose company was the largest grain miller in the world at the time, instituted one of the first large-scale employee profit-sharing schemes in the United States. He firmly believed that profit sharing was an effective tool to motivate workers, leading coworkers to be more responsible and practice effective self-management. Early examples also include the personal care company Procter and Gamble introducing broad-based employee profit sharing in 1887 and employee ownership some years later, and George Eastman of Eastman Kodak introducing broad-based profit sharing in 1912, followed by a form of employee ownership similar to stock options. In order to retain the kind of workers on which Kodak's rapid innovation and growth relied, he created what was the first stock option program in a high-tech corporation in the United States: if workers stayed with the company, they could keep their company shares, and they could purchase additional shares for $100 each and cash them in for almost $600 each.

Current Examples

Today, there are countless examples of extremely successful companies, across all sectors of the U.S. economy, that implement employee financial participation programs, including many of the nation's largest companies, such as General Motors, Exxon Mobil, IBM, Ford Motor Company, Apple Computers, Microsoft, Intel, Johnson and Johnson, United Parcel Service, Amazon, Coca-Cola, Cisco Systems, Google, and Morgan Stanley.

To focus on a few of these examples, the oil and energy company Exxon Mobil, the United States's largest corporation, has had broad-based employee ownership plans since John D. Rockefeller established one of the earliest and most generous employee ownership plans at

Standard Oil in 1919. General Motors, the country's fifth-largest corporation, which was bailed out and restructured, has cash profit sharing and broad-based stock options, while the health plan for its unionized workers and retirees encompasses a significant chunk of the company's stock. Ford Motor Company, the country's ninth-largest corporation, has an employee stock ownership plan and a deferred profit-sharing plan for its salaried and hourly employees, along with cash profit sharing, and the employees own over 13 percent of the company. Johnson and Johnson, the country's forty-second-largest corporation, has a long history of offering employees financial participation in the company as a result of the writings of Robert Wood Johnson II early in the twentieth century, and it has a significant employee stock ownership plan.

Broad-based employee financial participation is especially popular in the technology sector. Microsoft, a leader in software and the Internet, beginning in 1986 pioneered broad-based employee ownership in the software industry, and it has continually updated these benefits. It was ranked number 76 on *Fortune* magazine's "100 Best Companies to Work For" list in 2012. Apple Computers, the country's seventeenth-largest corporation, has a generous employee stock purchase plan that allows employees to buy up to $25,000 of the stock annually at a 15 percent discount; Apple employees who bought stock for the past seven years realized a reported 869 percent return on their investment. The computer chip company Intel, which was one of the pioneers in terms of offering broad-based employee ownership and having profit sharing in Silicon Valley, received the Global Equity Organization Award, both for its financial education of workers and for having the most effective ownership plan. At Google, all employees are equity holders; the company is about 5 percent owned by its nonexecutive employees and has reserved almost 5 percent of its shares for future stock and stock-option grants for its workforce. In 2012, Google won first place in *Fortune* magazine's "100 Best Companies to Work For" list, in part for its commitment to broad-based employee ownership.

The evidence is not limited to these firms. About 10 to 20 percent of the 4,500 corporations whose stock is traded on the New York Stock Exchange and the NASDAQ exchange have meaningful employee ownership. Among the Fortune 100, 21 companies have broad-based share ownership as part of their business cultures. These include firms in technology, finance, transportation, energy, retail, and consumer products. About 10 percent of companies in the Fortune 500 have employee stock ownership of between 5 and 20 percent. Some have employee stock purchase plans that allow workers to buy stock at a discount; others have lower-risk employee stock ownership plans that finance the purchase of stock for workers through loans or company contributions and grant stock to workers for which the workers do not pay. Sometimes, ESOP stock matches employee contributions to 401(k) plans. Some plans allow workers to use their wages to buy stock in 401(k) plans. Others have stock options or plans that grant workers restricted stock that they receive as long as they stay with the company.

Today, most full or majority employee ownership of a company is done through an ESOP. Workers receive grants of stock from their company that they do not have to purchase with savings or wages. Typically, the company sets up a trust that accumulates company stock for employees through company contributions or loans that the company takes out to buy the stock. A bank or other lender has to approve the loan, based on an evaluation of whether the company can pay it back. Because workers do not pay for the stock with their wages, this form of employee ownership has lower risk. Most ESOPs are not on stock exchanges, insulating them from the volatility of stock markets.

CURRENT PREVALENCE OF EMPLOYEE OWNERSHIP IN THE UNITED STATES

Evidence from the GSS

What is the prevalence of employee ownership in the United States today? How many workers share in the profits generated by corporations by having an ownership stake in the company where they work? What proportion of their companies do workers typically own?

It has been difficult to find comprehensive answers to these questions because of the dearth of data pertinent to employee ownership. National surveys did not include questions on this topic until, in 2002, a major effort by employee ownership researchers led to the inclusion of a set of questions on this topic in the General Social Survey (GSS). As noted in Chapter 1, the GSS, which is conducted by the National

Opinion Research Center at the University of Chicago, collects nationally representative data for the United States and therefore allows us to glean knowledge that is descriptive of the U.S. population as a whole.[3] The GSS began including the Topical Module on Shared Capitalism, with questions on the prevalence of employee ownership, in 2002. Since then, this module has been included in the GSS every four years: in 2006, 2010, and 2014.

As part of the Shared Capitalism Module, the GSS asks all workers if they are eligible for profit sharing (defined as bonuses that are affected by company performance), and asks private-sector workers about their ownership of employer stock (either directly or through a pension plan) and whether they hold stock options. As described in Chapter 1, there are several ways in which U.S. employees can get an ownership stake in the companies where they work, including grants to an ESOP, restricted stock grants, stock matches to employee 401(k) contributions, allocation of employer contributions to stock in deferred profit-sharing and other pension plans, and employee purchases of stock through 401(k) plans, employee stock purchase plans (ESPPs), or the open market.

Employees may also acquire an ownership stake in the companies where they work through stock options, which give them the right to purchase stock at a predetermined set price (strike price) regardless of the market price of the stock. So if the market price of the company's stock goes above the strike price, the owner of the stock can choose to exercise the stock option—i.e., exercise her right to buy at the exercise price and immediately sell at the market price, thereby making a profit. And if the stock price falls below the market price, the owner of the stock option can hold off on exercising the option so as not to lose money until the market price rises above the strike price. However, an important point is that stock-option holdings of employees can only be considered employee ownership if and when they are exercised. Thus, stock options could lead to employee ownership, but they do not strictly constitute employee ownership in and of themselves. Therefore, when we present descriptive statistics or figures on employee stock-option holdings, we will treat them as distinct from employee ownership.

Table 2.1 presents evidence on the prevalence of employee ownership in the United States since 2002 from the General Social Survey. According to the most recent GSS wave, which includes the shared capitalism module in 2014, 19.5 percent of employees at private-sector

Table 2.1 Participation in Employee Ownership and Stock Options, 2002–2014

	2002	2006	2010	2014
All private sector				
% of employees covered				
Own company stock	20.1	17.1	17.8	19.5
Hold stock options	12.3	9.1	9.0	7.2
Number of employees covered (millions)				
Total employees in economy[a]	109.0	114.5	107.7	117.3
Own company stock	21.9	19.6	19.2	22.9
Hold stock options	13.4	10.4	9.7	8.5
Sample sizes	1,261	1,172	795	885

[a] The figure for total private-sector employees comes from Bureau of Labor Statistics establishment data for July of the given year.
SOURCE: Based on the authors' analysis of the General Social Survey (GSS). Data come from the Shared Capitalism Module of the GSS, administered by the National Opinion Research Center at the University of Chicago.

firms in the United States participated in employee ownership through ownership of company stock, and 7.2 percent participated through ownership of company stock options (column 4). This amounts to 22.9 million employees with stock and 8.5 million with stock options, out of a total of 117.3 million employees in the private sector.

TRENDS IN THE PREVALENCE OF EMPLOYEE OWNERSHIP

Evidence from GSS

How have these figures been evolving during the past decade, which includes the Great Recession? GSS data on employee ownership have been collected since 2002, which gives us some idea about the evolution of employee ownership in the past 15 years. As can be seen in Table 2.1, the prevalence of employee stock ownership was greatest in 2002, declined in 2006, increased slightly in 2010, and increased again in 2014. Among all private-sector employees in 2002, one-fifth (20.1

percent) owned company stock, and that fraction fell to just over one-sixth of employees in 2006 (17.1 percent) and 2010 (17.8 percent), but then rose back to almost one-fifth of employees in 2014 (19.5 percent). The trend for stock options, however, has been consistently downward, from 12.3 percent of employees holding stock options in 2002 to 7.2 percent doing so in 2014. This latter trend largely reflects the scaling back of broad-based stock options after the requirement for expensing of stock options took effect starting in 2005 (Blasi, Freeman, and Kruse 2013).

Evidence from Pension Reports

We can also glean valuable information about the prevalence and evolution of employee ownership in the United States from the U.S. Department of Labor's Form 5500 firm pension records, which include all employee ownership held through ESOPs, 401(k) plans, deferred profit-sharing plans, and other defined contribution plans. As seen in Table 2.2, based on the Form 5500 data over time, the number of ESOP participants grew from 7.6 million in 1999 to 10.6 million in 2012, while the number of participants in 401(k) plans that hold employer stock declined from 7.3 million to 5.7 million, and the number in other defined contribution plans that hold employer stock declined from 0.6 to 0.2 million. The decline in participants in non-ESOP plans with employer stock reflects the scaling back of employee ownership through 401(k) plans following the Enron failure, in which workers used their own savings to overinvest in company stock. The total number of participants, including both ESOPs and non-ESOPs, nonetheless grew over this period from 15.6 million to 16.5 million. Employee ownership grew not just in number of participants but in coverage of the private-sector workforce. Using lower-bound estimates that count only the largest plan in each company (to eliminate any double counting of employees in more than one plan), the percentage of private-sector employees in pension plans with employer stock grew from 11.9 percent in 1999 to 14.9 percent in 2006, falling slightly to 14.4 percent in 2010 and 13.6 percent in 2012.

Much of the growth in ESOPs over this period has taken place in S corporations. In S corporations, corporate income or loss is passed through to shareholders, who then pay income tax based on those

Table 2.2 Employee Ownership through Pension Plans, 1999–2012

	1999	2002	2006	2010	2012
Number of participants					
ESOPs	7,653,578	9,204,622	9,786,398	10,289,126	10,553,875
Non-ESOP 401(k) plan with employer stock	7,332,699	8,722,121	8,613,102	6,418,207	5,744,207
Other DC plan with employer stock	572,582	589,152	265,189	209,788	183,853
Total	15,558,859	18,515,895	18,664,689	16,917,121	16,481,935
Number of employees (lower bound)[a]					
ESOPs	6,880,734	8,529,702	9,132,348	9,497,685	9,855,628
Non-ESOP 401(k) plan with employer stock	6,850,212	8,349,747	8,182,402	6,243,223	5,637,659
Other DC plan with employer stock	433,470	452,121	218,356	184,727	161,753
Total	13,104,578	16,150,879	17,195,112	15,599,622	15,396,508
% of private-sector workforce[b]					
ESOPs	6.2	7.8	7.9	8.8	8.7
Non-ESOP 401(k) plan with employer stock	6.2	7.7	7.1	5.8	5.0
Other DC plan with employer stock	0.4	0.4	0.2	0.2	0.1
Total	11.9	14.8	14.9	14.4	13.6

[a] Figures reflect only largest plan within company, eliminating any double counting of participants in more than one plan.
[b] Based on total private employment for December of given year, from the Bureau of Labor Statistics website, bls.gov.
SOURCE: Calculations based on microdata from the U.S. Department of Labor's (USDOL) Form 5500 pension database.

gains or losses (per Subchapter S of Chapter 1 of the Internal Revenue Code). A separate analysis of Form 5500 data finds that the number of ESOP participants in S corporations more than doubled, from 193,746 to 459,878, over the 2002–2009 period (Brill 2012), which represents more than half of the total growth in ESOP participants over this period. This growth occurred despite the fact that retiring owners in S Corporations are not currently eligible to avoid capital gains by selling to an ESOP (although there is currently a bipartisan bill in Congress to extend this tax benefit to S corporations).

Table 2.3 focuses on employee ownership in publicly traded U.S. firms with deferred employee ownership plans, using the core data on which the empirical analyses in Chapters 3 through 5 are based. The

Table 2.3 Employee Ownership in Pension Plans in Publicly Held Companies, 1999–2011

	1999	2002	2005	2008	2011
Share of firms reporting any EO stock in pension plans (%)	16.8	19.9	19.4	18.6	17.9
Share of workers at firm participating in EO in pension plans, on average (%)	13.4	21.9	17.5	17.2	14.3
Sample size	9,907	8,533	7,804	6,900	5,980

SOURCE: Data are from the USDOL Form 5500 pension database, matched to Standard and Poor's Compustat data on publicly traded companies in the United States.

percentage of publicly traded firms with deferred employee ownership plans grew from 16.8 percent in 1999 to 19.9 percent in 2002, then declined slightly to 19.0 percent in 2006 and 17.5 percent in 2010. Furthermore, the share of workers participating in employee ownership in pension plans at the typical firm grew from 11.0 percent in 1999 to 14.6 percent in 2002, then declined slightly to 13.6 percent in 2006 and to 12.6 percent in 2010. It is noteworthy that the levels of coverage are similar between publicly traded companies and the entire private-sector workforce.

Does the Prevalence of Employee Ownership at Firms Vary by Company Characteristics Like Industry, Size, and Worker Occupation?

Many people think that employee ownership is 1) held mainly by managerial workers, 2) used mainly in large firms, and 3) concentrated in the high-tech computer industry. While there is some validity in these generalizations, they fail to capture the broad prevalence of employee ownership in the U.S. economy. In fact, employee ownership is prevalent in many different industries and occupations, and it spans firms of all sizes. We can glean information about the firm size, industry, and occupation distribution of employee ownership from the GSS.

Figure 2.1 illustrates the share of workers who own stock in their company within specific industries, using combined data from the 2002, 2006, 2010, and 2014 waves of the GSS. As we can see, there is substantial participation in employee stock ownership among workers in

Figure 2.1 Employee Ownership by Industry

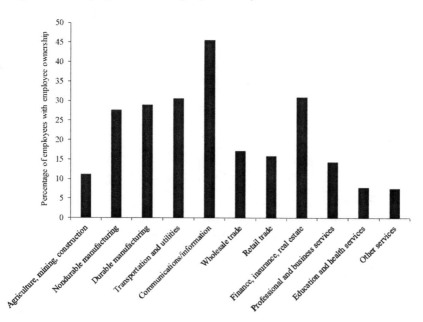

SOURCE: Based on combined data from the 2002, 2006, 2010, and 2014 GSS.

most industries. The communications and information industry has the highest prevalence of employee ownership, with over 45 percent of workers in that industry participating in employee ownership of stock. The finance, insurance, and real estate industry and the transportation and utilities industry have the next highest prevalence with 31 percent, closely followed by durable manufacturing with 29 percent and nondurable manufacturing with 28 percent of their workers participating in employee ownership of stock. Even apart from the leading industries, there is substantial employee ownership of stock across most other industries: wholesale trade has 17 percent; retail trade has 16 percent; professional and business services has 14 percent; agriculture, mining, and construction has 11 percent; and the two lowest industries are education and health services with 8 percent and other services with 7 percent.

Figure 2.2 analogously illustrates the share of workers who own stock options within industries. We see similar patterns here, though at lower levels generally. The communications and information indus-

Figure 2.2 Employees with Stock Options by Industry

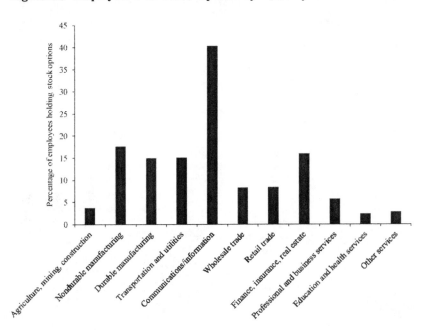

SOURCE: Based on combined data from the 2002, 2006, 2010, and 2014 GSS.

try is the clear leader with 40 percent of its employees holding stock options, and the lowest prevalence is among education and health services (2 percent) and other services (3 percent).

We next turn to an analysis of prevalence of employee ownership within occupations, again using combined data over the 2002–2014 waves. Figures 2.3 and 2.4 show that employee stock and stock option holdings are common across all occupations. As seen in Figure 2.3,

Figure 2.3 Employee Ownership by Occupation

NOTE: Managerial jobs include executives, legislators, administrators, and managers. Management-related jobs include accountants and auditors, underwriters, financial officers, management analysts, and personnel and labor specialists. Professional jobs include architects, engineers, mathematicians and statisticians, scientists, doctors and dentists, registered nurses, teachers, and lawyers. Technical jobs include laboratory technicians, dental hygienists, electrical technicians, and mechanical technicians. Sales jobs include sales workers, advertising sales workers, and cashiers. Clerical jobs include secretaries, stenographers, typists, administrative support jobs, telephone operators, and receptionists. Service jobs include firefighters, police, waiters, cleaners, cooks, and child-care workers. Agriculture jobs include farm operators and managers, farm workers, sea captains, and fishers. Blue-collar jobs include mechanics, equipment repairers, locksmiths, construction supervisors and workers, tailors, bakers, plant and machine operators, and bus and taxi drivers.
SOURCE: Based on combined data from the 2002, 2006, 2010, and 2014 GSS.

management-related occupations and managerial occupations had the greatest salience of employee stock ownership. Specifically, over 28 percent of workers in management-related occupations (which include accountants and auditors, financial officers, and management analysts, among others) had employee stock ownership. This figure was around 26 percent for managerial occupations (executives, managers, etc.), 24 percent for clerical occupations (secretaries, administrative support jobs, telephone operators, receptionists, etc.), 20 percent for sales occupations (sales workers, cashiers, etc.), and 19 percent for professional and technical occupations (engineers, architects, doctors, lawyers, laboratory technicians, electrical and mechanical technicians, etc.). Furthermore, blue-collar and agriculture occupations each had 17 percent of workers who were employee stock owners, and service occupations had 7 percent. Figure 2.4 illustrates stock option holdings within occupations, showing that the greatest concentration of stock option holdings

Figure 2.4 Employees with Stock Options by Occupation

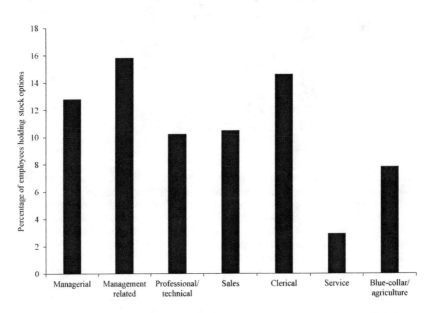

NOTE: See note for Figure 2.3.
SOURCE: Based on combined data from the 2002, 2006, 2010, and 2014 GSS.

is in management-related occupations (16 percent), followed by clerical occupations (15 percent) and managerial occupations (13 percent).

Finally, let us turn to an examination of employee ownership by firm size. Figures 2.5 and 2.6 illustrate that employee stock ownership is by no means only a large-firm phenomenon. While it is true that large firms have a greater share of workers who own stock and stock options in their company, there is substantial ownership at firms of all sizes. As seen in Figure 2.5, nearly 6 percent of workers owned stock at their firm in companies that number fewer than 10 employees in size, and 10 percent in companies that have 10–99 employees. This figure was nearly 19 percent at firms with 100–999 employees, nearly 24 percent at firms with 1,000–9,999 employees, and about 40 percent at firms with more than 10,000 employees. As for stock option holdings, Figure 2.6 shows that the share of workers holding stock options in their company was about 2 percent at firms with fewer than 10 employees, 4 percent at firms with 10–99 employees, 7 percent at firms with 100–999 employ-

Figure 2.5 Employee Ownership by Size of Firm

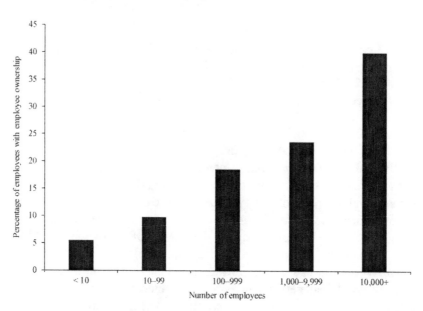

SOURCE: Based on combined data from the 2002, 2006, 2010, and 2014 GSS.

Figure 2.6 Employees with Stock Options by Size of Firm

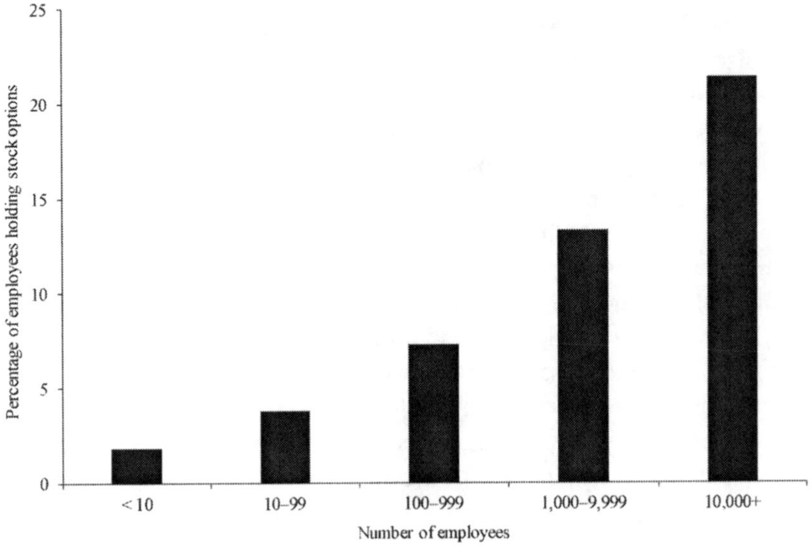

SOURCE: Based on combined data from the 2002, 2006, 2010, and 2014 GSS.

ees, 13 percent at firms with 1,000–9,999 employees, and 21 percent at firms with more than 10,000 employees.

Prevalence of Employee Ownership Abroad

Employee ownership is a common practice not only in the United States but also abroad. A study of Canadian and Australian firms (Long and Shields 2005) reports that 21 percent of firms in each of those countries use employee stock purchase plans, and 10 percent of firms in Canada and 3 percent of firms in Australia use employee stock options. As mentioned in Chapter 1, the European Union encouraged employee ownership in its four reports from 1991 to 2008 known as the PEP-PER (Promotion of Employee Participation in Profits and Enterprise Results) Reports and called on member states to promote participation by employed persons in profits and enterprise performance. A 2013 study gives an overview of employee ownership in 27 European Union Countries (Hashi and Hashani 2013). Using data from the European Company Survey and the European Working Conditions Survey, the authors show that the average proportion of companies offering employee share ownership in Europe in 2009 was around 6.5 percent. This is likely to be an understatement, because these surveys focus on small and medium-sized firms, and employee ownership tends to be more prevalent in large firms. The countries with the greatest prevalence of employee ownership are France, the Netherlands, Sweden, Denmark, the United Kingdom, and Romania, and the financial sector tends to be the industry with the highest prevalence across countries. Additionally, the proportion of employees involved in employee ownership has been growing during the 2000s in almost all countries in the EU. For example, the proportion of employees participating in employee ownership programs in France grew from around 3 percent in 2000 to around 7 percent in 2005 and 2010.

Data for the United Kingdom from the Workplace Employment Relations Survey's 2004 wave indicate that around 20 percent of British workplaces and 32 percent of British employees had some form of employee ownership scheme, which is comparable to rates in the United States (Bryson and Freeman 2010). There are various employee ownership structures in the United Kingdom that are different from those in the United States. For example, the United Kingdom has Save As You Earn (SAYE) Plans, which are all-employee plans that give workers tax breaks when they save to purchase their employer's shares but that do not require that they purchase the shares; Share Incentive Plans (SIP), which are all-employee schemes that offer tax breaks for employees holding shares in the company for which they work; and Company Share Option Plans (CSOPs), in which companies can grant chosen employees or directors up to 30,000 British pounds of tax- and national insurance–advantaged share options. The majority of the stock ownership plans are open to all nonmanagerial employees because the UK tax code usually requires this as a condition to be able to obtain tax breaks. The prevalence of share ownership in the United Kingdom has grown over time, partly reflecting the fact that the UK government has encouraged broad-based share ownership schemes through favorable tax treatment, especially in the 1980s, when many government tax incentives were introduced. In that decade, the conservative government of Margaret Thatcher gave tax advantages for profit-related pay. Since 1997, the more liberal Labour government has given tax advantages to share ownership schemes at the expense of profit-related schemes, which became fully taxable. Unlike the United States, which gives tax breaks for collective ownership of shares through ESOPs, the United Kingdom gives breaks for individual share ownership. Pendleton, Whitfield, and Bryson (2009) show that the proportion of private-sector UK workplaces with broad-based shared ownership grew from 20 percent in 1984 to 28 percent in 2004.

There is wide variation in the structures and incidence of employee share ownership in other industrialized countries (Kaarsemaker, Pendleton, and Poutsma 2010). Among European countries other than the United Kingdom, France has the highest incidence, with a well-developed employee savings system that allows employees to contribute bonuses and savings into employer stock (Fakhfakh, Pérotin, and Gago 2012). Relatedly, France also has substantial profit sharing as a result of government tax advantages offered to firms and employees for participation in profit sharing; one profit-sharing scheme is even compulsory in France for all firms with 50 employees or more (Pérotin and Robinson 2002). Germany has not traditionally promoted employee share ownership, and the incidence of employee share ownership is not as high as in the United States, the United Kingdom, or France, partly because of the prevalence of very large private companies, in which ownership is frequently dominated by large—and often hidden—owners. In Western Europe, the countries with the lowest use of employee share ownership have typically been the Mediterranean countries (Greece, Italy, Portugal, and Spain), though Spain and Italy have important representation in majority-worker-owned firms and worker cooperatives (Arando et al. 2015).

Russia and Eastern European countries have also had considerable employee ownership as a result of the transition from Soviet-style economies (Mygind et al. 2006). After an initial surge of interest and policies promoting employee ownership in Russia following the breakup of the Soviet Union (Blasi, Kroumova, and Kruse 1997), the Russian economy has returned to concentrated ownership (Kachalina 2013). During the 1990s in Eastern Europe, privatization of many enterprises that were formerly government owned often involved distributing shares at discounted prices to employees (Earle and Estrin 1998; Pérotin and Robinson 2002), and in some cases employees had priority rights to purchase their firm when it was privatized. Latin American countries also have considerable concentrations of employee share ownership (Burdin 2014).

As described in Chapter 1, employee ownership has been shown to have positive effects on employee performance, job satisfaction, morale, and workplace cooperation, among other outcomes. So, one might ask, why then isn't employee ownership more prevalent in the United States as well as globally?[4] One possibility is that many firms are simply not aware of the benefits, which would be understandable, given that the positive evidence has mostly accumulated only in the past two decades. An important complementary point is that while the evidence on economic performance is generally positive, it is also clear that there is no *automatic* positive effect of employee ownership, and many firms with employee ownership do not do well. Without a clear formula for success, firms will understandably be reluctant to adopt an organizational innovation like employee ownership, particularly when there may be significant fixed costs as well as a risk of raising employee expectations for changes in the way the company will operate and decisions will be made.

Firms will be especially reluctant to provide expanded ownership to employees if doing so dilutes the ownership stakes of existing owners—the dilution will need to be counteracted by improved performance, if existing owners are to have an incentive to distribute ownership more broadly. Existing owners may also be concerned about spreading financial information about the firm more broadly, since such information could fall into the hands of competitors. Finally, employee ownership may not be appropriate for all firms and workers, particularly those in volatile industries. Nevertheless, the growth in employee ownership in many countries indicates that the potential benefits may be increasingly recognized and may outweigh the barriers mentioned above.

Apart from reluctance by firms to adopt employee ownership, unions have often been opposed to employee ownership, in part because of the concern that it will complicate collective bargaining by blurring the line between workers and owners. Unions have also been concerned about financial risks to workers from variable pay and wealth, and about management's willingness to provide transparent, accurate information about the financial status of the company. Some unions, however, have taken initiatives to pursue employee ownership for workers out of a belief that this can improve workers' economic status, job security, and role in workplace governance.[5] The positive effects of employee ownership and other shared rewards on employee attitudes and behaviors appear to be just as strong among union workers as among nonunion workers (McCarthy et al. 2011).

In sum, there has been a substantial amount of experimentation with employee ownership around the globe in the past several decades. This chapter has also demonstrated that broad-based employee ownership is prevalent not just in a handful of firms, sectors, or occupations, but is an economy-wide phenomenon in the United States and has a long and rich history, with roots in the philosophies of America's founding fathers. Given this background, we are now ready to present in the next three chapters our results on the role played by employee ownership in employment stability and firm survival in the United States during the decade encompassing the Great Recession.

Notes

1. Indeed, the value of a firm's stock represents the present discounted value of its profits. Therefore, by owning firm stock, an employee has a claim to a share of those profits.
2. This section draws on material presented in Blasi, Freeman, and Kruse (2013).
3. The GSS is based on face-to-face interviews of randomly selected adults in their homes. Face-to-face interviews are generally superior to mail surveys, computer-assisted surveys, and telephone surveys in terms of accuracy. Moreover, the interviewer can ask more detailed questions than is possible under other survey methods, and the respondent can refer to personal records to answer questions more precisely. While response rates have been declining for telephone and mail surveys in recent years, the General Social Survey gets responses from more than 70 percent of the people who are asked to participate in the survey, which is very high in comparison to other surveys.
4. For a discussion of the specific barriers facing worker cooperatives, see Olsen (2013).
5. For a further description of the arguments and literature on this topic, and new evidence on the effects of employee ownership, profit sharing, and stock options for union workers, see McCarthy et al. (2011).

3
How Does Employee Ownership
Affect Employment Stability?

Understanding the determinants of employment stability during economic downturns is a topic of keen interest to academic researchers, government policymakers, and firms. In this chapter, we examine whether broad-based employee ownership affects employment stability within firms.

As described in Chapter 2, the prevalence of employee ownership has been growing over the past several decades in the United States and other advanced economies. According to the 2014 wave of the General Social Survey (GSS), 19.5 percent of U.S. workers own company stock, and 7.2 percent own company stock options. And according to data from the U.S. Department of Labor (USDOL) Form 5500 firm pension records, between 1999 and 2010 the share of publicly traded U.S. firms with employee ownership plans grew from 16.8 percent to 17.5 percent, and the share of workers participating in employee ownership at the typical such firm rose from 11.0 percent to 12.6 percent, on average. Given the increasing prevalence of employee ownership, along with the high economic and social costs that can accompany job loss, understanding the relationship between employee ownership and employment stability carries great policy significance.

Data from the GSS indicate that employee ownership and employment stability are positively correlated. As was shown in Chapter 1, involuntary layoffs and turnover intentions are lower among workers who are employee owners. Moreover, between 2006 and 2010, while the figures for EO workers remained relatively stable, layoffs and turnover intentions at non-EO firms grew. Put differently, layoffs and turnover became more likely among non-EO workers than among EO workers following the Great Recession. At the same time, job satisfaction was higher among EO workers than among non-EO workers.

In this chapter, we conduct an in-depth empirical analysis of how firms with employee ownership programs weathered the recessions of

2001–2003 and 2008–2010 in terms of employment stability relative to firms without employee ownership programs, and also of whether such firms were less likely to lay off workers when faced with negative shocks more broadly. In our econometric analyses, we use a rich array of measures of employee ownership at firms, including

- the presence of employee ownership stock in pension plans,
- the presence of employee stock ownership plans (ESOPs),
- the value of employee ownership stock per employee,
- the share of the firm owned by employees,
- the share of workers at the firm participating in employee ownership, and
- the share of workers at the firm participating in ESOPs.

We also consider both economy-wide negative shock measures (increases in the unemployment rate, declines in the employment-to-population ratio) and firm-specific negative shock measures (declines in firm sales, declines in firm stock price).

The firm data that we use to examine the relationship between employee ownership and employment stability come from Standard and Poor's Industrial Compustat database on publicly traded companies, matched to Form 5500 pension data collected by the USDOL, which contain detailed information on employee ownership in ESOPs and other defined contribution pension plans. These are administrative data for the population of publicly traded firms. This represents an improvement over data sets based on samples that are generally drawn from special surveys suffering from small sample sizes and bias from self-selection of respondents.[1] A further advantage is that we are able to follow firms over time, which allows us to use panel methods in our econometric analyses to help control for unobserved firm-specific effects. Our findings show strong evidence that employee ownership firms are less likely to reduce employment in the face of economy-wide and firm-specific negative shocks.

This examination constitutes an important contribution to the research on employee ownership and has important implications for government policymakers and employers. It presents large-scale empirical evidence on the role of employee ownership in employment stability during recessions. It also underscores the importance of government policy that encourages employee ownership as a policy tool to curb unemployment during recessions.

THEORETICAL FRAMEWORK

Why would we expect firms with employee ownership programs to exhibit greater employment security during economic downturns?

Firms often introduce employee ownership programs as a means of building a long-term cooperative employment relationship with their employees, and a lower incidence of layoffs can be a means of maintaining the credibility of the firm's commitment to that relationship. Employee ownership firms may provide greater employment security as part of an overall effort to build a more cooperative workplace culture and a sense of psychological ownership (Pierce, Rubenfeld, and Morgan 1991). This cooperative culture can increase worker effort, as well as create a general willingness on the part of workers to make adjustments during times of economic distress, both of which can increase firm productivity and lower the firm's need to lay off workers during downturns. Employee ownership can also increase firm revenues, as employees may be more willing to share technical information with management, which can increase production efficiency. Indeed, numerous empirical studies have linked employee ownership to increased productivity and other performance measures, as was reviewed in Chapter 1.

Apart from any effects that workplace culture may have on productivity, employee ownership may help to instill a sense of psychological ownership, which firms maintain in part through a commitment to preserve employee jobs. Such a workplace culture could increase employee willingness to invest in valuable firm-specific skills.

There may be a stabilizing effect of employee ownership if it increases the flexibility of compensation, although this is likely to occur only under special circumstances. While firms may contribute less company stock to employees during hard times, this flexibility is no different from what happens in other defined contribution pension plans in which the company contribution may vary year to year. Extra flexibility due to employee ownership would occur only if 1) employer stock substitutes for wages or other benefits and 2) the returns from employer stock (dividends and share price increase) are seen as part of employee compensation. When these conditions hold and negative demand shocks occur, the decrease in company stock value provides an automatic "pay cut" for workers, and the lower fixed component of pay (due to substitution of employee ownership for fixed pay) means that firms will have less incentive to lay off workers.[2]

PAST STUDIES ON EMPLOYEE OWNERSHIP AND EMPLOYMENT STABILITY

A number of past empirical studies examined related issues, and one of the goals of the current study is to update some of these earlier findings and understand how employee ownership firms weathered the recessions of the 2000s.

Pencavel and Craig (1992, 1994) studied the plywood worker cooperatives (companies in which 100 percent, or almost 100 percent, of the company's stock is held by its workers) in the U.S. Pacific Northwest and found that cooperatives kept employment stable but, instead, adjusted wages in response to a negative product price over the analysis window of 1968–1986. These results seem to be achieved without compromising efficiency, since productivity levels were 6–14 percent higher among the plywood cooperatives compared to conventional companies (Craig et al. 1995). Pencavel, Pistaferri, and Schivardi (2006) examined employment and wages at worker-owned and conventional enterprises in Italy using a matched employer-worker panel for 1982–1994 and, similarly, found that worker-owned firms had lower wages and more variable wages than conventional firms but also had less volatile employment. Numerous other studies using panel data on worker cooperatives from various countries in Europe and South America have found analogous results (Burdin and Dean 2009; Jones et al. 2013).

Blair, Kruse, and Blasi (2002) tracked U.S. public companies with broad-based employee ownership plans holding more than 17 percent of company stock over 1983–1995 and compared them to otherwise-similar firms in the same industries. They found that employee ownership was associated with greater employment stability, which did not come at the expense of firm efficiency, given that the stock market performance of the employee ownership firms was slightly better than that of other firms. Similarly, studies have found employee ownership to be associated with greater employment stability in a broader sample of U.S. public companies from 1988 to 2001 (Park, Kruse, and Sesil 2004), and in a sample of U.S. closely held companies from 1988 to 1999 (Blasi, Kruse, and Weltmann 2013).

There is some evidence suggesting that employees may exert formal or informal pressures to increase job security in employee ownership firms. For example, a majority of Americans say that if they owned company stock and an outside investor was attempting a takeover, they would not sell, even for twice the market value of the stock (Kruse and Blasi [1999], citing a 1994 EBRI/Gallup poll). This appears to be due to concerns that an outside investor would lay off workers (Kruse, Freeman, and Blasi 2010).

DATA AND METHODOLOGY

The firm data for this project were drawn from two sources: 1) Standard and Poor's Industrial Compustat database on publicly traded companies and 2) the Form 5500 pension plan data collected by the USDOL. The Compustat data comprise information on firm characteristics including total employment and financial information, while the Form 5500 pension plan data set contains detailed information on employee ownership in ESOPs and other defined contribution pension plans. We matched firm records from the Compustat data and Form 5500 data using each firm's unique IRS Employer Identification Number for the 13 years spanning 1999–2011, resulting in the firm-year panel data set on which all of our analyses are based.

Our data set is composed of the full population of publicly traded companies in the United States. As noted earlier, this data set provides an advantage over data sets drawn from special surveys suffering from small sample sizes and self-selection of respondents. It also allows us to conduct longitudinal analyses in order to help control for unobserved firm-specific effects. Furthermore, the data span a decade when the United States experienced two recessions, in 2001 and 2008, allowing us to examine how employee ownership firms weathered these economic downturns relative to nonemployee ownership companies. We also have an array of measures of employee ownership at companies, including the presence of employee ownership through pension programs and ESOPs, and the extent of such employee ownership in terms of total participation and share of the firm owned by workers.

Our goal is to understand whether firms with employee ownership programs exhibit greater employment stability in the face of economic downturns. We examine six different measures of employee ownership within firms in our empirical analyses in particular:

1. Any employee ownership: whether a firm reported any employee ownership stock in any of its defined contribution pension plans, including employee ownership in 401(k) plans, ESOPs, and deferred profit-sharing plans in a given year.[3]

2. ESOP: whether a firm reported having an ESOP plan in a given year.

3. Employee ownership stock value per employee at the firm: total employee-owned stock value in dollars, divided by total number of employees (including nonowners) at a firm in a given year.[4]

4. Percentage of company owned by employees: the share of the firm owned by employees in a given year.

5. Employee owners as a percentage of employees: the share of all employees participating in employee ownership at a firm in a given year.

6. ESOP participants as a percentage of employees: the share of all employees participating in ESOPs at a firm in a given year.

To understand how firms with employee ownership programs respond to economic downturns, we first consider a fairly broad proxy of economic conditions—namely, the unemployment rate. Figure 3.1 illustrates trends in the national unemployment rate during 1999–2011. The recessions starting in 2001 and 2008 are clearly seen in this figure as sustained increases in the unemployment rate (from 3.97 percent in 2000 up to 5.99 percent in 2003, and from 4.62 percent in 2007 up to 9.63 percent in 2010).

Figure 3.1 Average Unemployment Rate, 1999–2011

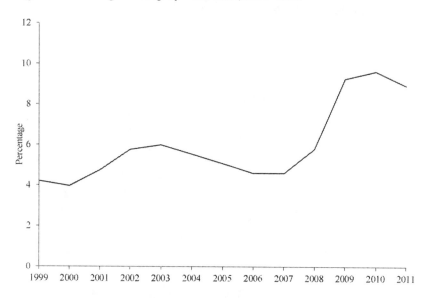

SOURCE: Based on labor force statistics from the Current Population Survey season-
ally adjusted unemployment rate for ages 16 and older.

As a first step in understanding how firms with employee ownership
vary their employment with changes in the unemployment rate, we plot
in Figure 3.2 the average yearly percentage change in employment over
2000–2010 at firms with and without any employee ownership in their
defined contribution plans. As the figure clearly illustrates, employment
was more stable at firms with employee ownership than at firms without during 2000–2010: employment declines were smaller at employee
ownership firms during years when overall employment shrunk across
firms; employment increases were also smaller at employee ownership
firms during years with overall employment growth across all firms.
This trend is also evident in Panels B and C of Figure 3.2, which illustrate yearly percentage change in employment at firms with and without ESOPs, and at firms with and without at least 5 percent of the firm
owned by employees. Note that the threshold of 5 percent meets the
Security and Exchange Commission's definition of a major stakeholder.

Figure 3.2   Average Yearly Percentage Change in Employment by Employee Ownership, 2000–2010

Panel A: Percentage change in employment by "Any employee ownership" (firm reported any EO stock)

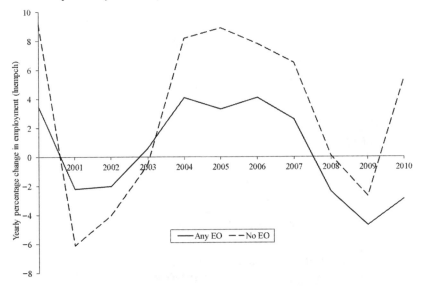

Panel B: Average yearly percentage change in employment by ESOP status

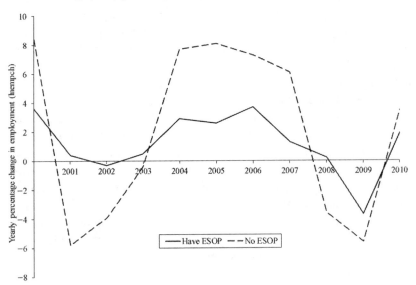

Figure 3.2 (continued)

Panel C: Average yearly percentage change in employment for companies with greater than 5 percent employee ownership and companies with less than 5 percent employee ownership

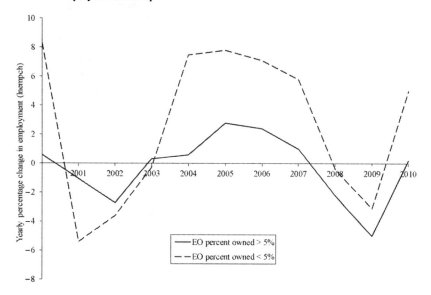

SOURCE: Based on authors' calculations from the USDOL Form 5500 pension database.

Although Figure 3.2 illustrates the basic story, we would like to know whether the positive relationship between employment stability and employee ownership holds when we control for firm characteristics. We therefore estimate standard regressions, estimating the relationship between the yearly percentage change in employment at firms and each of our six measures of employee ownership when the firm faces negative demand shocks. We use two *economy-wide* measures of demand shocks—1) unemployment rate and 2) employment-to-population ratio. Changes in the employment-to-population rate may serve as a better measure of economic downturn than the unemployment rate, because the latter counts individuals who are not working but seeking employment, which is often difficult to measure accurately. We also examine employment stability in the face of two types of *firm-level* negative shocks: 1) decline in firm sales since the previous year and 2) decline in firm stock price since the previous year.

In our regressions we control for firm characteristics, including capital stock growth (to control for mergers and divestitures), union status (to control for union-influenced employment stability), interactions between demand shocks and average firm size (to control for differential response between larger and smaller firms), industry and industry-specific trends, and firm fixed effects (to control for time-invariant firm characteristics).[5] In our regressions, we focus on employee ownership as of the prior year so that we can be more sure that the employee ownership was a plausible cause rather than effect of the demand shocks.

While our basic method controls for any general differences among firms in their employment growth or decline (through the fixed effects), it is nonetheless possible that the responsiveness to demand shocks may vary among firms in a way that affects our estimates. For example, some firms may have developed methods of avoiding layoffs when negative demand shocks occur, and these firms may be more likely to adopt employee ownership. In this case the employee ownership would be more of a symptom than a cause of reduced layoffs. We can test this possibility by analyzing firms that switched employee ownership status within the period, through either adopting or dropping employee ownership, and comparing their response to negative demand shocks when they do and do not have employee ownership. To implement this test, for each of the demand shocks we identify companies in our sample that experienced at least one negative shock with, and one negative shock without, employee ownership.[6] While this sample is limited, it allows us to explore whether the same firm appears to act differently when it does and does not have employee ownership.

To streamline the exposition of results, we have summary tables with key findings representing the estimated implied percentage changes in firm employment in response to each of the types of demand shocks. These summaries are based on regressions presented in the appendix.

EMPIRICAL ANALYSIS

Table 3.1 depicts descriptive statistics by presence of employee ownership programs, and it illustrates, among other results, that EO firms were on average larger, grew more slowly than non-EO firms, were more likely to be unionized as indicated by a union pension plan, and were more likely to be in the transportation and finance industries, while less likely to be in the service industry, than non-EO firms. These differences by employee ownership status indicate the importance of controlling for these characteristics in our estimates, since stability may be influenced by firm size, union status, and industry trends. Within the employee ownership firms, the average dollar value of employee ownership stock per employee was $10,540, the share of the firm owned by employees was 3.3 percent, and the share of workers at the firm participating in employee ownership was 72 percent.

The extent of employee ownership within firms is explored in more detail in Table 3.2. There is considerable variation in employee ownership assets per employee, with a "low" value (twenty-fifth percentile) of $949, a "high" value (seventy-fifth percentile) of $12,967, and a "very high" value (ninety-fifth percentile) of $44,414. (Note that these are averages across all employees in the firm, not just those owning stock.) Since these are publicly held companies, most of the stock is held by outside shareholders. Employees typically own just a small percentage of these companies, with a median of 1.5 percent and a ninety-fifth percentile of 11.9 percent, indicating that in only 5 percent of the EO companies do employees own about one-eighth or more of the company. There is less variation in the employee coverage measures, for which Table 3.2 shows that employee owners are four-fifths (80.2 percent) of all employees in the median EO firm, and ESOP participants are three-fourths (74.6 percent) of all employees in the median ESOP firm. This broad coverage is not surprising, given that our employee ownership measure is based on Form 5500 data for pension plans, which are required to be broad-based to qualify for tax deductibility.

Table 3.3 summarizes the results from the regressions examining the percentage change in within-firm employment in response to negative shocks (based on the full regression estimates reported in Tables 3A.1 through 3A.4). The first column summarizes the results from the

Table 3.1 Descriptive Statistics on Public Company Sample

	Any employee ownership			No employee ownership		
	Mean	Std. dev.	Obs.	Mean	Std. dev.	Obs.
Employee size	14,128	60,808	18,620	4,185	20,544	67,276
Employment change (natural logarithm)	0.012	0.213	16,814	0.025	0.347	55,987
ESOP	0.350	0.477	18,620	0.000	0.000	67,276
EO assets per employee ($)	10,540	16,195	18,429	0.000	0.000	67,276
EO as % of firm ownership	0.033	0.056	17,395	0.000	0.000	59,092
Employee owners as % of all employees	0.721	0.283	18,620	0.000	0.000	67,276
ESOP participants as % of all employees	0.229	0.366	18,620	0.000	0.000	67,276
Sales ($ millions)	4,186	16,416	18,611	1,181	6,057	67,071
Sales change (natural logarithm)	0.056	0.252	16,743	0.091	0.460	53,050
Sales change if increase	0.160	0.182	11,372	0.289	0.373	34,566
Sales change if decrease	−0.164	0.237	5,371	−0.279	0.371	18,440
Stock price change (%)	−0.040	0.573	16,333	−0.128	0.842	50,983
Stock price change if increase	0.333	0.332	8,635	0.491	0.517	23,926
Stock price change if decrease	−0.450	0.508	7,664	0.682	0.680	26,758
Capital stock change (natural logarithm)	0.055	0.443	13,639	0.078	1.265	48,790
Union pension plan	0.210	0.408	18,620	0.055	0.228	67,276
Agriculture, forestry, fishing	0.004	0.060	18,620	0.003	0.054	67,276
Mining	0.034	0.181	18,620	0.043	0.203	67,276
Construction	0.011	0.104	18,620	0.009	0.092	67,276

Manufacturing	0.372	0.483	18,620	0.375	0.484	67,276
Transportation, communications, and utilities	0.112	0.315	18,620	0.092	0.289	67,276
Wholesale trade	0.029	0.168	18,620	0.031	0.172	67,276
Retail trade	0.070	0.255	18,620	0.050	0.217	67,276
Finance, insurance, and real estate	0.251	0.434	18,620	0.187	0.390	67,276
Service	0.114	0.318	18,620	0.196	0.397	67,276
Public administration	0.003	0.056	18,620	0.015	0.122	67,276

SOURCE: Data are from USDOL Form 5500 pension database matched to Standard and Poor's Industrial Compustat data on publicly traded companies in the United States.

Table 3.2 Amounts of Employee Ownership within Employee Ownership Firms

	Low (25th percentile) (1)	Median (50th percentile) (2)	High (75th percentile) (3)	Very high (95th percentile) (4)	Average (5)	Number of firm-year observations (6)
EO assets per employee[a] ($)	949	3,937	12,967	44,414	10,540	18,429
EO as % of firm ownership	0.5	1.5	3.9	11.9	3.3	17,395
Employee owners as % of all employees	52.5	80.2	100.0	100.0	72.4	18,539
ESOP participants as % of all employees	47.6	74.6	96.9	100.0	68.8	7,515

NOTE: Restricted to years in which firm had positive values of employee ownership. EO = employee ownership.
[a] Calculated across all employees in company, not just participants in employee ownership plan.
SOURCE: Data are from USDOL Form 5500 pension database matched to Standard and Poor's Industrial Compustat data on publicly traded companies in the United States.

specification in which the negative shock measure we use is increased unemployment rate, the second column uses decreased employment-to-population ratio, the third column uses decreased firm sales, and the final column uses decreased stock price.

Unemployment Rate

Our first set of results, presented in column 1 of Table 3.3, indicates support for our hypothesis that employee ownership firms reduce their employment by a smaller percentage when faced with a negative shock compared to firms without employee ownership.

When the unemployment rate increases by 1.0 percent, firms without employee ownership in any of their defined contribution plans decrease employment by 3.0 percent, while firms with any employee ownership in their defined contribution plans decrease employment by only 2.8 percent, and firms with any ESOPs decrease employment by only 1.7 percent. The second of these differences is strong enough to reject ran-

Table 3.3 Summary of Overall Relationship between Employee Ownership and Employment Stability

Negative shock:	% change in company employment in response to negative demand shocks			
	Unemployment rate up 1%	Economy employment rate down 1%	Firm sales down 10%	Firm stock price down 10%
No employee ownership	−3.0	−4.2	−4.0	−0.7
Any employee ownership	−2.8	−3.9	−4.0	**−1.0**
Any ESOP	**−1.7**	**−2.7**	−3.2	−1.0
Average EO assets per employee ($)				
Zero	**−3.0**	**−4.2**	**−3.8**	**−0.7**
Mean (10,540)	**−2.1**	**−3.1**	**−2.9**	**−0.5**
Low (947)	**−2.9**	**−4.1**	**−3.7**	**−0.7**
Median (3,937)	**−2.7**	**−3.8**	**−3.4**	**−0.6**
High (12,967)	**−2.0**	**−2.8**	**−2.7**	**−0.5**
Very high (44,414)	**0.6**	**0.4**	**−0.3**	**0.1**
By % of company owned by employees				
Zero	−3.0	−4.2	−3.7	**−0.7**
Mean (3.3)	−2.9	−4.1	−3.8	**−0.7**
Low (0.5)	−3.0	−4.2	−3.7	**−0.7**
Median (1.5)	−2.9	−4.1	−3.8	**−0.7**
High (3.9)	−2.9	−4.0	−3.8	**−0.7**
Very high (11.9)	−2.6	−3.7	−4.1	**−0.9**
By % of workers in EO				
Zero	**−3.0**	**−4.2**	−3.6	−0.7
Mean (72.4)	**−2.3**	**−3.3**	−3.3	−0.8
Low (52.5)	**−2.5**	**−3.6**	−3.4	−0.8
Median (80.2)	**−2.3**	**−3.2**	−3.3	−0.8
High (100)	**−2.1**	**−3.0**	−3.2	−0.9
By % of workers in ESOP				
Zero	**−3.0**	**−4.1**	**−3.7**	−0.7
Mean (68.8)	**−1.4**	**−2.2**	**−2.2**	−0.5
Low (47.6)	**−1.9**	**−2.8**	**−2.6**	−0.6
Median (74.7)	**−1.3**	**−2.0**	**−2.0**	−0.5
High (96.9)	**−0.8**	**−1.4**	**−1.6**	−0.4
Very high (100)	**−0.7**	**−1.3**	**−1.5**	−0.4

NOTE: Based on regression results reported in Appendix Tables 3A.1 to 3A.4. Figures in bold are based on statistically significant employee ownership × negative shock interactions (at the 95% level).

SOURCE: Data from USDOL Form 5500 pension database matched to Standard and Poor's Industrial Compustat data on publicly traded companies in the United States.

dom sampling error as an explanation. We see a statistically stronger relationship when we turn our attention to the value of employee ownership stock per employee at the firm: when the unemployment rate increases by 1 percent, firms where the value of employee ownership assets per worker is low (where "low" is defined as being at the twenty-fifth percentile of the distribution) decrease their employment by 2.9 percent, in contrast to firms where the value of employee ownership is at the median (fiftieth percentile), high (seventy-fifth percentile), or very high (ninety-fifth percentile) levels, at which employment declines by only 2.7 percent, 2.0 percent, and 0.6 percent, respectively. Employment declines are only statistically weakly related to the percentage of the firm owned by employees, but they are statistically strongly related to employee coverage: when the unemployment rate increases by 1 percent, firms where the share of workers in employee ownership is zero, low, at the median, and high experience an employment decrease of 3.0 percent, 2.5 percent, 2.3 percent, and 2.1 percent, respectively. Likewise, firms in which the share of workers in ESOPs is zero, low, at the median, high, and very high experience an employment decrease of 3.0 percent, 1.9 percent, 1.3 percent, 0.8 percent, and 0.7 percent, respectively.

Employment-to-Population Ratio

As mentioned before, changes in the employment-to-population rate serve as a better measure of economic downturn than the unemployment rate because the latter considers individuals who are not working but are seeking employment, which can be difficult to measure accurately. Therefore, we also estimate all our regressions treating as our indicator of economic downturn a decline in the annual employment-to-population rate rather than an increase in the annual unemployment rate. Figure 3.3 illustrates the trajectory of the employment-to-population rate over the period 1999–2011.

The results summarized in column 2 of Table 3.3, using the employment-to-population ratio, show strong evidence that EO firms provide greater employment security than non-EO firms during economic downturns.

Firms with no employee ownership experience a 4.2 percent employment decline when the employment-to-population rate goes

Figure 3.3 Average Employment-to-Population Rate, 1999–2001

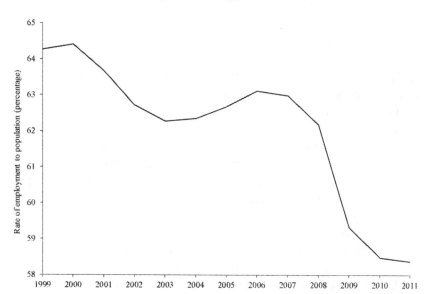

SOURCE: Based on labor force statistics from the Current Population Survey season-
ally adjusted employment-to-population rate for ages 16 and older.

down by 1.0 percent, in contrast to firms with employee ownership,
in which employment decreases by only 3.9 percent, and firms with
ESOPs, in which employment decreases by 2.7 percent. Once again,
only the second difference is strong enough to reject sampling error.
Firms with zero, low, median, and high EO assets per employee reduce
employment by 4.2 percent, 4.1 percent, 3.8 percent, and 2.8 percent,
respectively (while the estimate for very high EO assets per employee
is actually a 0.4 percent increase in employment). Again, the pattern
is favorable but statistically weak when examining share of the company owned by workers, while it is favorable and statistically strong
when examining employee coverage in any EO or in ESOPs. When
the employment-to-population ratio goes down by 1.0 percent, firms
with zero, low, median, and high shares of employees who are owners reduce their employment by 4.2 percent, 3.6 percent, 3.2 percent,
and 3.0 percent, respectively, and firms with zero, low, median, high,
and very high shares of workers in ESOPs reduce their employment

by 4.1 percent, 2.8 percent, 2.0 percent, 1.4 percent, and 1.3 percent, respectively.

Decline in Firm Sales

We next examine employment stability in the face of firm-level negative shocks using two specific measures: 1) decline in firm sales since the previous year and 2) decline in firm stock price since the previous year. Column 3 of Table 3.3 summarizes our regression findings on the extent to which firms with EO programs exhibit smaller employment declines when they experience a 10 percent decrease in their sales. Here we find fewer statistically strong relationships with EO measures than when we use the economy-wide measures of demand shocks. The strongest findings occur with respect to two areas: 1) EO assets per employee and 2) percentage of workers in an ESOP. A 10 percent decrease in sales is linked to a 3.3 percent decline in employment when EO assets per employee are zero. When these assets are at their low, median, high, and very high values, the employment declines are 3.3 percent, 3.0 percent, 2.3 percent, and 0.1 percent, respectively. Similarly, as the share of employees who are ESOP participants increases, the employment decline drops from 3.3 percent when no workers are covered to 1.1 percent when all workers are covered.

Decline in Firm Stock Price

As with the sales measure, the stock price measure provides fewer strong relationships between EO and employment declines than do the economy-wide measures. The one measure showing a favorable relationship is EO assets per employee: when a firm's stock price declines by 10 percent, firms with zero EO assets per employee have an employment decline of 0.7 percent. This employment decline is reduced to 0.6 percent and 0.5 percent at the median and high levels of EO assets per employee and essentially disappears at the very high level. There is a puzzling but small positive relationship between employment declines and the percentage of the company owned by employees, indicating that the employment decline is 0.7 percent at low levels but 0.9 percent at very high levels of percentage of company owned. A caution on this result, however, is that it appears to be sensitive to the specification, and the result disappears when we add prior employment change or take out the interactions between firm size and demand shocks as predictors. (Also, the results for other measures become more favorable to the stabilizing effect of EO, but here we present the results from the base specification for the sake of consistency.)

PROBING ALTERNATIVE SPECIFICATIONS

There are a variety of ways in which the regressions testing for employment stability can be specified. Our investigation of a number of alternative specifications produced the same general pattern of results.[7] One key issue is causality: does employee ownership lead to stability, or do more stable firms adopt employee ownership? This can be examined in part by examining the responses of the same firms before and after they adopt or drop employee ownership. Since we are focused on the effects of negative demand shocks, we break out companies (called "EO switchers") that experienced at least one negative demand shock with employee ownership and one without employee ownership. If employee ownership firms are simply more stable to begin with (before adopting employee ownership), there should be no difference in their EO and non-EO years, while there should be a difference if employee ownership plays a plausible role in employment stability.

A total of 391 firms met our criteria to be EO switchers for the economy-wide measures (that is, they experienced at least one recession year with employee ownership and one without employee ownership), while for the firm-specific measures of sales and stock price, 376 and 536 firms, respectively, met our criteria as EO switchers. While these are not large samples and there may be other unobserved factors at work, these firms can nonetheless shed light on the role of employee ownership in stability.

Table 3.4 summarizes the results from studying these switchers (based on fuller results presented in Appendix Tables 3A.5–3A.8). As shown in column 1, when they did not have employee ownership, their average response to an increase in the unemployment rate was a 2.1 percent decline in employment, while having average EO assets per employee is linked to only a 1.4 percent decline and having the

Table 3.4 Summary of Changes in Employment Stability for Employee Ownership Switchers

Negative shock	% change in company employment in response to negative demand shocks			
	Unemployment rate up 1%	Economy employment rate down 1%	Firm sales down 10%	Firm stock price down 10%
Response of non-EO firms	−3.1	−4.3	−3.3	−0.7
Responses of EO switchers during time that they had:				
No employee ownership	−2.1	−3.1	−3.5	−0.6
Any employee ownership	−2.7	−3.9	−3.4	**−1.0**
ESOP	−1.6	−2.3	−2.6	−0.8
Mean of EO assets/employee	**−1.4**	**−2.6**	**−2.5**	−0.6
Mean of % of company owned by employees	−2.8	−3.8	−3.6	**−0.9**
Mean of % of workers in EO	−2.5	−3.5	−3.3	**−1.0**
Mean of % of workers in ESOP	**−1.3**	**−2.2**	**−1.5**	−0.7

NOTE: "Switchers" = firms that adopted or dropped employee ownership and had negative demand shocks during periods both with and without employee ownership. Based on regression results reported in Appendix Tables 3A.5–3A.8. Figures in bold are based on statistically significant employee ownership × negative shock × switcher interactions (at the 95% level).

SOURCE: Data are from USDOL Form 5500 pension database matched to Standard and Poor's Industrial Compustat data on publicly traded companies in the United States.

mean percentage of workers in an ESOP is linked to only a 1.3 percent decline. These two EO measures show similar results when the negative demand shock is measured as a decrease in the employment/population ratio (column 2) or a 10 percent decrease in firm sales (column 3). The results for other EO measures in columns 1–3 are mixed, but none are strong enough to reject sampling error. In addition, none of the results for stock price in column 4 showed increased stability as firms switched to employee ownership, while three replicate the puzzling result noted in Table 3.3 of employee ownership being linked to greater employment responses to stock price declines. One potential difficulty with the stock price measure is that it reflects investor evaluations of future profitability, and as such it is sensitive to firm news such as increased layoffs. So it may be that the stock price decrease is a response to announcements of employment cutbacks rather than an exogenous predictor of declines in demand for the firm's products.

Therefore, the analysis of EO switchers points to possible changes in employment behavior as firms adopt employee ownership, particularly with regard to the measures of EO assets per employee and percentage of workers in an ESOP.

We further probed the results in three ways. First, we used the lagged change in logarithm of employment as a control, to address possible correlations between unobserved variables and the lagged dependent variable as identified by Arellano and Bond (1991). The results using the Arellano-Bond correction were actually slightly more favorable to the stabilizing effect of employee ownership than the results we present here. Second, we omitted change in capital stock as a control variable, since that is potentially endogenous with respect to determination of the employment level. This omission, however, made no noteworthy difference in our results of interest. Third, we omitted the interactions between firm size and the demand shocks, which made no difference in the estimates using the economy-wide demand shocks but weakened the results using the sales measure. We believe it is appropriate to control for these interactions since employee ownership firms are larger on average (as shown in Table 3.1), and larger firms have larger proportional responses to sales decreases (as shown in Appendix Table 3A.3). Overall, we find that results from these additional tests are broadly consistent with the results presented here.

CONCLUSION

Using data matched between USDOL Form 5500 and the Industrial Compustat database on all publicly traded U.S. companies during 1999–2011, this chapter has shown that firms with employee ownership are linked to greater employment stability in the face of an economic downturn when measured as macroeconomic negative shocks (increases in the unemployment rate, decreases in the employment-to-population ratio) as well as firm-specific negative shocks (declines in firm sales). The size of the effects varies by employee ownership measure, with favorable results most consistently found for average EO assets per employee, employee owners as a percentage of all employees, and ESOP participants as a percentage of all employees. While we have only limited data to examine changes in employment behavior as firms adopt or drop employee ownership, our tests point to increased stability for firms that switch employee ownership status when they have high EO assets per employee or a high percentage of employees covered by an ESOP.

These findings highlight the role that employee ownership may play in stabilizing employment, particularly during recessions. They also underscore the importance of government policy that encourages employee ownership as a policy tool to curb unemployment during recessions, as we will discuss in the final chapter.

Notes

1. Our data do not contain firms with employee ownership that are not publicly traded, either because they are privately held or because they are completely employee owned.
2. This dynamic would be similar to the theorized effect of profit sharing on employment stability proposed by Weitzman (1984), since the short-run marginal cost of labor would be lower than the marginal revenue product of labor, leading firms to retain workers.
3. Note that this measure understates employee ownership in pension plans because it does not include employee ownership in master trusts or collective trusts that combine assets of several plans.
4. Note that this will be understated when employee ownership stock is held in master trusts or collective trusts that combine assets of several plans.
5. Specifically, we estimate the following ordinary least squares specification, which illustrates the magnitude of employment changes in response to changes in the unemployment rate at EO firms as compared to non-EO firms:

$$LNEMPCH_{it} = \beta_0 + \beta_1 NegD_{it} + \beta_2 PosD_{it} + \beta_3 NegD_{it} \times EO_{it-1} + \beta_4$$
$$PosD_{it} \times EO_{it-1} + \beta_5 \times NegD_{it} \times Avgemp_i + \beta_6 PosD_{it} \times Avgemp_i +$$
$$X_{it} + \theta_i + \varepsilon_{it} ,$$

where

$LNEMPCH_{it} = \ln(\text{employment})$ at firm i in year $t -\ln(\text{employment})$ at firm i in year $t - 1$, winsorized at the first and ninety-ninth percentiles to reduce the influence of extreme values.

EO_{it-1} = employee ownership variable at firm i in year $t - 1$, alternatively measured as 1) dummy for any employee ownership, 2) dummy for ESOP, 3) average employee-owned stock per employee in dollars (across all employees, not just participants), 4) proportion of company owned by employees, 5) employee owners as proportion of all employees, and 6) ESOP participants as proportion of all employees.

$NegD_{it}$ = Negative demand shock from $t - 1$ to t, alternatively measured as 1) percentage-point increase in the U.S. unemployment rate, 2) percentage-point decrease in the U.S. employment/population ratio, 3) decrease in firm ln(sales), and 4) percentage decrease in firm stock price. This variable takes the value 0 if there was no negative demand shock.

$PosD_{it}$ = Positive demand shock from $t - 1$ to t, alternatively measured as 1) percentage-point decrease in unemployment rate, 2) percentage-point increase in employment/population ratio, 3) increase in ln(sales), and 4) percentage increase in stock price. This variable takes the value 0 if there was no positive demand shock.

$Avgemp_i$ = Mean of ln(employment) within firm across all reported years.

X_{it} = vector of firm controls for firm i in year t, including capital stock growth, presence of collectively bargained pension plan, industry dummies, and linear and quadratic industry-specific time trends (Industry $i \times t$ and Industry $i \times t^2$).

θ_i = firm fixed effects.

Our hypothesis is that $\beta_1 < 0$ and $\beta_3 > 0$—i.e., employment will decline by a smaller percentage at EO firms than at non-EO firms in response to negative demand shocks (with the decrease in employment being β_3 percent smaller in magnitude at EO firms than at non-EO firms).

We exclude the $EO_{it} - 1$ main effect since 1) any general differences in employment changes between EO and non-EO firms will be captured by the firm fixed effects and 2) the responsiveness of firms to demand shocks may be affected by their changes in employment growth associated with EO, so that an EO main effect would partly capture the stabilizing effect we are trying to estimate. We nonetheless include EO main effects in supplementary regressions and obtained similar results.

To probe the robustness of results, we use year dummies in place of the time trends, with similar results for the coefficient estimates on the interaction between the demand shock and employee ownership.

6. The estimating equation for this specification is:

$$
\begin{aligned}
LNEMPCH_{it} = {} & \beta_0 + \beta_1\, NegD_{it} + \beta_2\, PosD_{it} + \beta_3\, NegD_{it} \times EOswitcher_i \\
& + \beta_4 \times PosD_{it} \times EOswitcher_i + \beta_5\, NegD_{it} \times EOswitcher_i \times EO_{it-1} \\
& + \beta_6\, PosD_{it} \times EOswitcher_i \times EO_{it-1} \\
& + \beta_7 \times NegD_{it} \times EOnonswitcher_i \times EO_{it-1} \\
& + \beta_8\, PosD_{it} \times EOnonswitcher_i \times EO_{it-1} + \beta_9 \times NegD_{it} \times Avgemp_i \\
& + \beta_{10} PosD_{it} \times Avgemp_i + X_{it} + \theta_i + \varepsilon_{it} \,,
\end{aligned}
$$

where

EOswitcher$_i$ = Firm i had at least one negative demand shock with, and one without, employee ownership.

EOnonswitcher$_i$ = Firm i had employee ownership but did not meet the standard for EOswitcher$_i$. All other variables as defined in previous note.

$\beta_1 + \beta_3 + \beta_9(\text{Avgemp}_i)$ measures the response to negative demand shocks for switchers when they do not have employee ownership, and β_5 measures any change in response to negative demand shocks when switchers have employee ownership.

7. A sample of these results is available in our working paper Kurtulus and Kruse (2016).

Appendix 3A
Tables

72

Table 3A.1 Employment Responses to General Demand Shocks: Unemployment Rate

	(1)	(2)	(3)	(4)	(5)	(6)
Negative demand shock: UR increase	-0.029***	-0.030***	-0.02994***	-0.030***	-0.030***	-0.030***
	(0.002)	(0.001)	(0.00137)	(0.001)	(0.001)	(0.001)
Positive demand shock: UR decrease	0.065***	0.060***	0.05711***	0.061***	0.059***	0.059***
	(0.006)	(0.005)	(0.00533)	(0.006)	(0.006)	(0.005)
Negative shock interacted with:						
Any EO	0.002					
	(0.002)					
ESOP		0.014***				
		(0.003)				
EO assets per employee			0.00081***			
			(0.00010)			
EO % of company				0.037		
				(0.036)		
EO share of employees					0.009***	
					(0.003)	
ESOP share of employees						0.023***
						(0.004)
Positive demand shock interacted with:						
Any EO	-0.024**					
	(0.009)					
ESOP		-0.002				
		(0.012)				
EO assets per employee			0.00121***			
			(0.00036)			

EO % of company			-0.184*		
			(0.104)		
EO share of employees				0.001	
				(0.012)	
ESOP share of employees					0.005
					(0.015)
Negative demand shock × average firm ln(employment)	0.001	0.00070	0.001	0.001	0.001
	(0.001)	(0.00071)	(0.001)	(0.001)	(0.001)
Positive demand shock × average firm ln(employment)	-0.011***	-0.01271***	-0.012***	-0.012***	-0.012***
	(0.003)	(0.00276)	(0.003)	(0.003)	(0.003)
Firm and industry controls	Yes	Yes	Yes	Yes	Yes
Firm fixed effects	Yes	Yes	Yes	Yes	Yes
Observations	61,241	61,120	54,915	61,241	61,241
R-squared	0.125	0.12478	0.123	0.125	0.125
Number of firms	8,356	8,355	7,752	8,356	8,356

NOTE: The dependent variable = ln(employment change, winsorized). UR = unemployment rate. Fixed effects (within) regressions. Robust standard errors in parentheses. * significant at the 0.10 level; ** significant at the 0.05 level; *** significant at the 0.01 level. Firm and industry controls include collective bargaining status, change in capital stock, and industry trend and trend squared.

SOURCE: Data are from USDOL Form 5500 pension database matched to Standard and Poor's Industrial Compustat data on publicly traded companies in the United States.

Table 3A.2 Employment Responses to General Demand Shocks: Employment/Population Ratio

	(1)	(2)	(3)	(4)	(5)	(6)
Negative demand shock: E/Pop decrease	-0.040***	-0.041***	-0.04165***	-0.042***	-0.042***	-0.041***
	(0.002)	(0.002)	(0.00163)	(0.002)	(0.002)	(0.002)
Positive demand shock: E/Pop increase	0.122***	0.109***	0.10306***	0.106***	0.110***	0.107***
	(0.011)	(0.010)	(0.00952)	(0.010)	(0.010)	(0.010)
Negative shock interacted with:						
Any EO	0.003					
	(0.003)					
ESOP		0.015***				
		(0.004)				
EO assets per employee			0.00102***			
			(0.00013)			
EO % of company				0.044		
				(0.042)		
EO share of employees					0.012***	
					(0.004)	
ESOP share of employees						0.028***
						(0.005)
Positive demand shock interacted with:						
Any EO	-0.064***					
	(0.017)					
ESOP		-0.032				
		(0.020)				
EO assets per employee			0.00129**			
			(0.00064)			

	(1)	(2)	(3)	(4)	(5)	(6)
EO % of company				−0.580***		
				(0.184)		
EO share of employees					−0.026	
					(0.022)	
ESOP share of employees						−0.027
						(0.028)
Negative demand shock × average firm ln(employment)	0.002**	0.001	0.00156*	0.001	0.001*	0.001
	(0.001)	(0.001)	(0.00086)	(0.001)	(0.001)	(0.001)
Positive demand shock × average firm ln(employment)	−0.010**	−0.013***	−0.01479***	−0.014***	−0.013***	−0.014***
	(0.005)	(0.005)	(0.00479)	(0.005)	(0.005)	(0.005)
Firm and industry controls	Yes	Yes	Yes	Yes	Yes	Yes
Firm fixed effects	Yes	Yes	Yes	Yes	Yes	Yes
Observations	61,241	61,241	61,120	54,915	61,241	61,241
R-squared	0.125	0.125	0.12547	0.123	0.125	0.125
Number of firms	8,356	8,356	8,355	7,752	8,356	8,356

NOTE: The dependent variable = ln(employment change, winsorized). Fixed effects (within) regressions. Robust standard errors in parentheses. * significant at the 0.10 level; ** significant at the 0.05 level; *** significant at the 0.01 level. Firm and industry controls include collective bargaining status, change in capital stock, and industry trend and trend squared.

SOURCE: Data are from USDOL Form 5500 pension database matched to Standard and Poor's Industrial Compustat data on publicly traded companies in the United States.

Table 3A.3 Employment Responses to Firm-Specific Demand Shocks: Sales Changes

Negative demand shock: sales decrease	−0.357***	−0.362***	−0.37486***	−0.371***	−0.364***	−0.365***
	(0.017)	(0.016)	(0.01554)	(0.017)	(0.017)	(0.015)
Positive demand shock: sales increase	0.374***	0.366***	0.36387***	0.382***	0.368***	0.364***
	(0.012)	(0.011)	(0.01094)	(0.012)	(0.011)	(0.011)
Negative shock interacted with:						
Any EO	0.004					
	(0.031)					
ESOP		0.081*				
		(0.043)				
EO assets per employee			0.00781***			
			(0.00127)			
EO percent of company				−0.285		
				(0.420)		
EO share of employees					0.048	
					(0.037)	
ESOP share of employees						0.217***
						(0.048)
Positive demand shock interacted with:						
Any EO	−0.059***					
	(0.022)					
ESOP		−0.024				
		(0.040)				
EO assets per employee			−0.00023			
			(0.00088)			

	(1)	(2)	(3)	(4)	(5)	(6)
EO % of company				-0.322		
				(0.372)		
EO share of employees					-0.032	
					(0.028)	
ESOP share of employees						0.014
						(0.052)
Negative demand shock × average firm ln(employment)	-0.047***	-0.049***	-0.05168***	-0.050***	-0.049***	-0.049***
	(0.006)	(0.005)	(0.00533)	(0.006)	(0.005)	(0.005)
Positive demand shock × average firm ln(employment)	0.055***	0.053***	0.05286***	0.059***	0.054***	0.053***
	(0.004)	(0.004)	(0.00408)	(0.004)	(0.004)	(0.004)
Firm and industry controls	Yes	Yes	Yes	Yes	Yes	Yes
Firm fixed effects	Yes	Yes	Yes	Yes	Yes	Yes
Observations	58,553	58,553	58,442	52,435	58,553	58,553
R-squared	0.224	0.224	0.22455	0.222	0.224	0.224
Number of firms	8,126	8,126	8,125	7,524	8,126	8,126

NOTE: The dependent variable = ln(employment change, winsorized). Demand shocks measured as change in ln(sales), winsorized. Fixed effects (within) regressions. Robust standard errors in parentheses. * significant at the 0.10 level; ** significant at the 0.05 level; *** significant at the 0.01 level. Firm and industry controls include collective bargaining status, change in capital stock, and industry trend and trend squared.

SOURCE: Data are from USDOL Form 5500 pension database matched to Standard and Poor's Industrial Compustat data on publicly traded companies in the United States.

Table 3A.4 Employment Responses to Firm-Specific Demand Shocks: Stock Price Changes

	(1)	(2)	(3)	(4)	(5)	(6)
Negative demand shock: stock price decrease	−0.061***	−0.067***	−0.07030***	−0.068***	−0.065***	−0.069***
	(0.004)	(0.004)	(0.00369)	(0.004)	(0.004)	(0.004)
Positive demand shock: stock price increase	0.007	0.002	−0.00212	0.003	0.003	0.000
	(0.005)	(0.004)	(0.00407)	(0.004)	(0.005)	(0.004)
Negative shock interacted with:						
Any EO	−0.032***					
	(0.008)					
ESOP		−0.022*				
		(0.012)				
EO assets per employee			0.00171***			
			(0.00063)			
EO % of company				−0.149***		
				(0.045)		
EO share of employees					−0.021*	
					(0.011)	
ESOP share of employees						0.008
						(0.015)
Positive demand shock interacted with:						
Any EO	−0.032***					
	(0.010)					
ESOP		−0.016				
		(0.013)				
EO assets per employee			0.00358***			
			(0.00108)			

79

	(1)	(2)	(3)	(4)	(5)	(6)
EO % of company				-0.142		
				(0.107)		
EO share of employees					-0.016	
					(0.013)	
ESOP share of employees						0.017
						(0.019)
Negative demand shock × average firm ln(employment)	0.015***	0.014***	0.01333***	0.014***	0.014***	0.014***
	(0.002)	(0.002)	(0.00172)	(0.002)	(0.002)	(0.002)
Positive demand shock × average firm ln(employment)	-0.003	-0.005**	-0.00554***	-0.005**	-0.004**	-0.005**
	(0.002)	(0.002)	(0.00205)	(0.002)	(0.002)	(0.002)
Firm and industry controls	Yes	Yes	Yes	Yes	Yes	Yes
Firm fixed effects	Yes	Yes	Yes	Yes	Yes	Yes
Observations	56,389	56,389	56,283	54,907	56,389	56,389
R-squared	0.134	0.134	0.13424	0.134	0.134	0.134
Number of firms	7,807	7,807	7,806	7,751	7,807	7,807

NOTE: The dependent variable = ln(employment change, winsorized). Demand shocks measured as change in ln(stock price), winsorized. Fixed effects (within) regressions. Robust standard errors in parentheses. * significant at the 0.10 level; ** significant at the 0.05 level; *** significant at the 0.01 level. Firm and industry controls include collective bargaining status, change in capital stock, and industry trend and trend squared.

SOURCE: Data are from USDOL Form 5500 pension database matched to Standard and Poor's Industrial Compustat data on publicly traded companies in the United States.

Table 3A.5 Employment Ownership Switchers and General Demand Shocks: Unemployment Rate

UR increase	−0.030***	−0.030***	−0.030***	−0.030***	−0.031***	−0.030***
	(0.002)	(0.001)	(0.001)	(0.001)	(0.002)	(0.001)
UR increase × (EO switcher)	0.010*	0.005	0.006	0.006	0.009*	0.005
	(0.005)	(0.004)	(0.004)	(0.004)	(0.005)	(0.004)
UR increase × (EO switcher) ×						
Any EO	−0.006					
	(0.006)					
ESOP		0.010				
		(0.006)				
EO % of company			−0.083			
			(0.071)			
EO assets per employee				0.001***		
				(0.000)		
EO share of employees					−0.003	
					(0.008)	
ESOP share of employees						0.018**
						(0.007)
UR increase × (EO nonswitcher) ×						
Any EO	0.004					
	(0.003)					
ESOP		0.015***				
		(0.004)				
EO % of company			0.054			
			(0.037)			

	(1)	(2)	(3)	(4)	(5)
EO assets per employee			0.001*** (0.000)		
EO share of employees				0.013*** (0.004)	
ESOP share of employees					0.027*** (0.005)
Firm controls	Yes	Yes	Yes	Yes	Yes
Firm fixed effects	Yes	Yes	Yes	Yes	Yes
Observations	61,241	61,241	60,000	61,120	61,241
R-squared	0.125	0.125	0.124	0.125	0.125
Number of firms	8,356	8,356	8,281	8,355	8,356
Number of EO switchers	391	391	391	391	391
Number of EO nonswitchers	1,444	1,444	1,444	1,444	1,444

NOTE: The dependent variable = ln(employment change, winsorized). "EO switcher" = company had at least 1 EO and 1 non-EO observation in years when stock price declined. "EO nonswitcher" = other EO companies. Robust standard errors in parentheses. * significant at the 0.10 level; ** significant at the 0.05 level; *** significant at the 0.01 level. Control variables include collective bargaining status; change in capital stock; industry trends and trend squared; unemployment increase and its interaction with the EO switcher, the EO switcher times each EO measure, and the EO nonswitcher; and average ln(employment) interacted with unemployment increases and decreases.

SOURCE: Data are from USDOL Form 5500 pension database matched to Standard and Poor's Industrial Compustat data on publicly traded companies in the United States.

Table 3A.6 Employment Ownership Switchers and General Demand Shocks: Employment/Population Ratio

	(1)	(2)	(3)	(4)	(5)	(6)
E/pop decrease	-0.042***	-0.042***	-0.041***	-0.042***	-0.043***	-0.042***
	(0.002)	(0.002)	(0.002)	(0.002)	(0.002)	(0.002)
E/pop decrease × (EO switcher)	0.012**	0.006	0.006	0.006	0.012**	0.006
	(0.006)	(0.005)	(0.005)	(0.005)	(0.006)	(0.005)
E/pop decrease × (EO switcher) ×						
Any EO	-0.008					
	(0.007)					
ESOP		0.014*				
		(0.007)				
EO % of company			-0.069			
			(0.088)			
EO assets per employee				0.001***		
				(0.000)		
EO share of employees					-0.005	
					(0.009)	
ESOP share of employees						0.022**
						(0.009)
E/pop decrease × (EO nonswitcher) ×						
Any EO	0.005					
	(0.003)					
ESOP		0.017***				
		(0.004)				
EO % of company			0.059			
			(0.043)			

	(1)	(2)	(3)	(4)	(5)
EO assets per employee			0.001*** (0.000)		
EO share of employees				0.016*** (0.004)	
ESOP share of employees					0.033*** (0.006)
Firm controls	Yes	Yes	Yes	Yes	Yes
Firm fixed effects	Yes	Yes	Yes	Yes	Yes
Observations	61,241	60,000	61,120	61,241	61,241
R-squared	0.125	0.125	0.125	0.125	0.126
Number of firms	8,356	8,281	8,355	8,356	8,356
Number of EO switchers	391	391	391	391	391
Number of EO nonswitchers	1,444	1,444	1,444	1,444	1,444

NOTE: The dependent variable = ln(employment change, winsorized). E/pop = employment/population ratio. "EO switcher" = company had at least 1 EO and 1 non-EO observation in years when stock price declined. "EO nonswitcher" = other EO companies. Robust standard errors in parentheses. * significant at the 0.10 level; ** significant at the 0.05 level; *** significant at the 0.01 level. Control variables include collective bargaining status; change in capital stock; industry trends and trend squared; E/pop decrease and its interaction with the EO switcher, the EO switcher times each EO measure, and the EO nonswitcher; and average ln(employment) interacted with E/pop increases and decreases.

SOURCE: Data are from USDOL Form 5500 pension database matched to Standard and Poor's Industrial Compustat data on publicly traded companies in the United States.

84

Table 3A.7 Comparing Employment Responses among Employee Ownership Switchers across Sales Decreases

Sales decrease	-0.346***	-0.351***	-0.347***	-0.362***	-0.353***	-0.354***
	(0.017)	(0.015)	(0.015)	(0.015)	(0.016)	(0.015)
Sales decrease × (EO switcher)	-0.024	-0.017	-0.027	-0.040	-0.017	-0.023
	(0.052)	(0.047)	(0.047)	(0.042)	(0.053)	(0.046)
Sales decrease × (EO switcher) ×						
Any EO	0.017					
	(0.063)					
ESOP		0.080				
		(0.091)				
EO % of company			0.418			
			(1.012)			
EO assets per employee				0.009***		
				(0.002)		
EO share of employees					0.023	
					(0.081)	
ESOP share of employees						0.289***
						(0.080)
Sales decrease × (EO nonswitcher) ×						
Any EO	-0.006					
	(0.032)					
ESOP		0.066				
		(0.050)				
EO % of company			-0.717*			
			(0.410)			

EO assets per employee			0.007***		
			(0.001)		
EO share of employees				0.047	
				(0.038)	
ESOP share of employees					0.193***
					(0.058)
Firm controls	Yes	Yes	Yes	Yes	Yes
Firm fixed effects	Yes	Yes	Yes	Yes	Yes
Observations	58,553	57,327	58,442	58,553	58,553
R-squared	0.222	0.223	0.223	0.222	0.223
Number of firms	8,126	8,052	8,125	8,126	8,126
Number of EO switchers	376	376	376	376	376
Number of EO nonswitchers	1,475	1,475	1,475	1,475	1,475

NOTE: The dependent variable = ln(employment change, winsorized). "EO switcher" = company had at least 1 EO and 1 non-EO observation in years when stock price declined. "EO nonswitcher" = other EO companies. Robust standard errors in parentheses. * significant at the 0.10 level; ** significant at the 0.05 level; *** significant at the 0.01 level. Control variables include collective bargaining status; change in capital stock; industry trends and trend squared; sales increase and its interaction with the EO switcher, the EO switcher times each EO measure, and the EO nonswitcher; and average ln(employment) interacted with sales increases and decreases.

SOURCE: Data are from USDOL Form 5500 pension database matched to Standard and Poor's Industrial Compustat data on publicly traded companies in the United States.

Table 3A.8 Employee Ownership Switchers and Firm-Specific Demand Shocks: Stock Price Decreases

Stock price decrease	−0.060***	−0.062***	−0.063***	−0.065***	−0.064***	−0.064***
	(0.004)	(0.004)	(0.004)	(0.004)	(0.004)	(0.004)
Stock price decrease × (EO switcher)	0.006	−0.012	−0.011	−0.013	0.003	−0.012
	(0.013)	(0.010)	(0.010)	(0.010)	(0.012)	(0.010)
Stock price decrease × (EO switcher) ×						
Any EO	−0.038***					
	(0.014)					
ESOP		−0.003				
		(0.017)				
EO % of company			−0.145***			
			(0.042)			
EO assets per employee				0.002		
				(0.002)		
EO share of employees					−0.040**	
					(0.019)	
ESOP share of employees						0.016
						(0.023)
Stock price decrease × (EO nonswitcher) ×						
Any EO	−0.020**					
	(0.010)					
ESOP		−0.040**				
		(0.016)				
EO % of company			−0.124			
			(0.100)			

	(1)	(2)	(3)	(4)	(5)
EO assets per employee			0.001*** (0.001)		
EO share of employees				−0.002 (0.013)	
ESOP share of employees					−0.004 (0.018)
Firm controls	Yes	Yes	Yes	Yes	Yes
Firm fixed effects	Yes	Yes	Yes	Yes	Yes
Observations	53,867	53,377	53,771	53,867	53,867
R-squared	0.112	0.112	0.112	0.112	0.112
Number of firms	7,585	7,577	7,584	7,585	7,585
Number of EO switchers	536	536	536	536	536
Number of EO nonswitchers	1,247	1,247	1,247	1,247	1,247

NOTE: The dependent variable = ln(employment change, winsorized). "EO switcher" = company had at least 1 EO and 1 non-EO observation in years when stock price declined. "EO nonswitcher" = other EO companies. Robust standard errors in parentheses. * significant at the 0.10 level; ** significant at the 0.05 level; *** significant at the 0.01 level. Control variables include collective bargaining status; change in capital stock; industry trends and trend squared; stock price increase and its interaction with the EO switcher, the EO switcher times each ln(employment) measure, and the EO nonswitcher; and average ln(employment) interacted with sales increases and decreases.

SOURCE: Data are from USDOL Form 5500 pension database matched to Standard and Poor's Industrial Compustat data on publicly traded companies in the United States.

4

Do Employee Ownership Firms Survive Recessions Better than Other Firms?

In this chapter, we turn our attention to the relationship between employee ownership and firm survival. Firm survival is an important outcome variable to examine, as it is generally an indicator of success for a company, increases job security for workers employed, and thereby benefits the economy more broadly by reducing unemployment and economic hardship. It therefore also constitutes an important component of any comprehensive analysis of employment stability.

What are the channels through which employee ownership may enhance firm survival? There are five possible channels:

As discussed in Chapter 2, previous research has shown employee ownership to be linked to increased firm and worker productivity through greater employee cooperation, commitment, and information sharing at the workplace. Despite the free-rider problem associated with group-based pay, studies have generally found employee ownership to be linked to higher performance (Doucouliagos 1995; Kaarsemaker 2006; Kruse and Blasi 1997; O'Boyle, Patel, and Gonzalez-Mulé, forthcoming).

1) Prior research has shown that employee ownership policies tend to be implemented along with other complementary high-performance workplace practices, such as employee involvement in decision making, team production, and on-the-job training, to create a more engaged workplace, which can also contribute to improved survival outcomes in the face of financial distress (Becker and Huselid 1998; Blasi et al. 2010; DeVaro and Kurtulus 2010; Ichniowski et al. 1996; Ichniowski, Shaw, and Prennushi 1997; Kurtulus, Kruse, and Blasi 2011).[1]

2) Employee ownership can reduce workplace conflict, which can contribute to production frictions and firm failure (Cramton, Mehran, and Tracy 2008).

3) Employee ownership tends to foster long-term employment relationships, which in turn encourage both employers and employees to make higher investments in firm-specific skills and facilitate increased productivity and survival prospects (Levine and Parkin 1994).

4) Employee ownership may increase employee willingness to suggest and participate in innovations that enhance long-term firm performance and prospects (Kruse, Freeman, and Blasi 2010).

On the other hand, employee ownership may negatively impact firm survival if it contributes to increased communication friction among employees or otherwise creates conflicts or inefficiencies within firms that can lead to a higher rate of failure. There may be especially strong potential for conflict and collective action problems when employees have heterogeneous preferences, such as may occur when there are substantial shares of employees in different occupations or divisions of a firm (Hansmann 1996). For example, if employees in each division favor increased investment in their own division, there may be complicated political conflicts in deciding where investment will occur. This concern primarily applies to cases where employees have strong roles in corporate governance, unlike the situation in most U.S. employee ownership companies.

For our examination of the link between employee ownership and firm survival, we use data on the entire universe of publicly traded U.S. companies as of 1999, following them through 2010. We use the same data set as in Chapter 3, based on merging two sources: 1) federal Form 5500 data, which is collected by the U.S. Department of Labor (USDOL) and provides information on employee participation in employee ownership through pension plans, and 2) Standard and Poor's Compustat data, which provide information on firm closures, mergers, acquisitions, and liquidations, as well as firm financial data. We estimate Cox hazard regressions predicting the probability of firm dissolution as a function of a wide array of measures of employee ownership and firm controls.[2]

PAST STUDIES ON EMPLOYEE OWNERSHIP AND FIRM SURVIVAL

Previous research on the relationship between employee ownership and firm survival is limited. Research on U.S. data shows that firms with employee ownership have higher survival rates. Blair, Kruse, and Blasi (2002) find that firms with 5 percent or more employee ownership stakes in 1983 were 20 percent more likely than closely matched industry pairs to survive through 1995. Park, Kruse, and Sesil (2004) examined publicly traded companies in the United States between 1998 and 2001 using hazard regression methods. They find that the firms in which employees owned 5 percent or more of the firm's stock were 21 percent more likely to survive through 2001. Welbourne and Cyr (1999) show that among companies with initial public offerings in 1988, those with broad-based ownership had higher rates of survival and stock-price growth.

The most recent study closest to ours is that of Blasi, Kruse, and Weltmann (2013), which uses a sample of closely held companies (without any publicly traded stock) from Dun and Bradstreet, in which ESOP companies were matched to non-ESOP companies in the same industry over the 1988–1999 period. This study finds that closely held ESOP companies in 1988 were only half as likely as non-ESOP firms to go bankrupt or close over the 1988–1999 period, and only three-fifths as likely to disappear for any reason. ESOP companies had significantly higher postadoption annual employment and sales growth, along with higher sales per employee. They were also four times more likely than their non-ESOP pairs to have defined benefit pension plans and other forms of defined contribution plans, which along with other data on the above-market compensation levels of most ESOPs indicates that greater survival does not come from lower labor costs.

Evidence from outside the United States focuses on worker cooperatives. Burdin (2014) finds that worker cooperatives in Uruguay exhibited death rates that were 29 percent lower than conventional firms. Pérotin (1987) finds that a shorter supply of capital funds is associated with future closure of cooperatives, while the business cycle appears to have similar effects on the failure rate of cooperatives and conventional firms. The pattern of risk for new firms, however, is found to be different: new cooperatives have a honeymoon period when commitment is high and risk of closure is lower than that for conventional firms, although risks increase later on (Pérotin 1997).

The Mondragon system of cooperatives in Spain also deserves mention here. The Mondragon Corporation is the largest worker cooperative in the world; it consists of a federation of worker cooperatives in the Basque region of Spain. While there have not been studies focused on survival of individual cooperatives in Mondragon, the survival and growth of the overall system since the 1950s is consistent with the idea that employee ownership can promote survival. The survival of the Mondragon system is undoubtedly enhanced by a supportive infrastructure that includes a university providing graduates and technical assistance to the cooperatives, and a bank providing financial capital and assistance with financial planning.

DATA AND METHODOLOGY

As described in Chapter 3, we compiled the data set by merging Standard and Poor's Industrial Compustat database on publicy traded firms and the Form 5500 pension plan data collected by the U.S. Department of Labor for the years 1999–2010. The Compustat database provides information on firm characteristics like total employment, industry, financial information, and reason for firm failure, while the Form 5500 pension plan database contains detailed information on employee ownership in defined contribution plans and employee stock option plans (ESOPs). We matched firm records from the Compustat data and Form 5500 data, using each firm's unique IRS employer identification number.

Also as described in Chapter 3, our data set is made up of the full sample of publicly traded companies in the United States, which is an important improvement over data sets drawn from special surveys suffering from small sample sizes and bias from self-selection of respondents. A further advantage is the 12-year span of our data set, covering a decade when the United States experienced two recessions, in 2001 and 2008; this allows us to examine how employee ownership firms weathered these economic downturns relative to nonemployee ownership companies. We also have a rich array of measures of employee ownership at companies, including the presence of employee ownership through pension programs and ESOPs, and the extent of such employee ownership in terms of total participation and the share of the firm owned by workers. One limitation is that firm disappearance is uncommon in general, especially among firms that have gone public. While we have enough disappearances to enable meaningful analysis, the low likelihood of disappearance makes it more difficult to establish significant differences, which makes any significant differences we do find all the more noteworthy. It should also be noted that our results are based on the universe of publicly traded companies over this time period, but that they might not fully generalize to closely held companies, which are generally smaller and have a different industrial distribution.

We estimate Cox proportional hazards regressions to predict the likelihood of firm failure.[3] The main independent variable of interest in our hazard models is the employee ownership variable. Our hypothesis is that the relative hazard ratio for this variable should be between zero and one, indicating a lower "hazard" or likelihood of failure for EO firms than non-EO firms, on average. The regressions also include firm controls, including firm size, union status, and industry.

We first estimate regressions in which we treat any disappearance of a firm from the Compustat database as a firm failure. However, companies may disappear as independent entities when they merge or are acquired by another company, and this can actually signal success in some cases, as other firms want to acquire or merge with successful companies. Compustat provides reasons for deletion of firms that no longer appear in that database, including acquisition, merger, bankruptcy, and liquidation. We therefore also estimate models in which firm failure is defined strictly as bankruptcy or liquidation.

As in the analysis of employment stability, we consider six different measures of employee ownership in our empirical analyses: 1) any employee ownership, 2) presence of an ESOP, 3) employee ownership stock per employee, 4) employee ownership—percentage owned, 5) employee owners as a percentage of employees, and 6) ESOP participants as a percentage of employees.

Table 4.1 shows average probabilities of firm disappearance by presence of employee ownership in the pooled analysis sample, and it illustrates that firms with employee ownership programs are less likely

Table 4.1 Firm Disappearance by Presence of Employee Ownership

	Mean (%)	Obs.	Mean (%)	Obs.
	Any employee ownership		No employee ownership	
Disappeared for any reason	5.2	17,981	7.6	77,874
Disappeared because of bankruptcy or liquidation	0.2	17,981	0.4	77,874
	Have ESOP		No ESOP	
Disappeared for any reason	4.9	8,027	7.4	87,828
Disappeared because of bankruptcy or liquidation	0.2	8,027	0.4	87,828
	EO% of company owned > 5%		EO% of company owned < 5%	
Disappeared for any reason	4.9	3,342	7.2	92,513
Disappeared because of bankruptcy or liquidation	0.2	3,342	0.4	92,513

NOTE: "Disappeared for any reason" = dummy variable equaling 1 if firm i in year t dropped out of the data set for any reason (including bankruptcy, merger/acquisition, liquidation, reverse acquisition, no longer publicly traded, no longer files with SEC); 0 otherwise. "Disappeared because of bankruptcy or liquidation" = dummy variable equaling 1 if firm i in year t went bankrupt or was liquidated; 0 otherwise.
SOURCE: Data are from USDOL Form 5500 pension database, matched to Standard and Poor's Compustat data on publicly traded companies in the United States, 1999–2011.

to disappear for any reason and also less likely to disappear because of bankruptcy or liquidation. The likelihood of disappearance for any reason in a given year is 5.2 percent for firms with any employee ownership and 7.6 percent for firms with no employee ownership, while the likelihood of disappearance due to bankruptcy or liquidation is 0.2 percent for firms with any employee ownership and 0.4 percent for firms with no employee ownership. These differences are similar when we compare firms with more than 5 percent of the company owned by employees and those with less than 5 percent employee ownership.

Figure 4.1 illustrates failure rates through 2010 among firms that were observed and either had or did not have employee ownership in 1999.[4] The two lines in each panel represent the share of 1999 firms that disappeared in each ensuing year, by presence of any employee ownership in 1999.[5] As seen in Panel A, the share of firms that disappeared was lower among firms that had employee ownership in 1999 than among those that did not have employee ownership, until the year 2005, after which the shares were nearly the same. This pattern is simi-

Figure 4.1 Failure Rates of 1999 Firms by Employee Ownership

Panel A: Failure rates by presence of any employee ownership in 1999

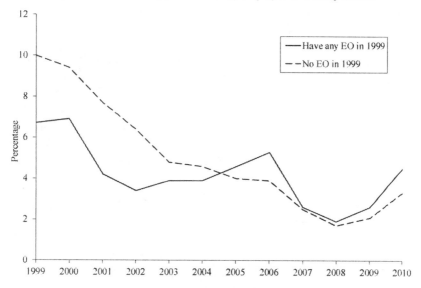

NOTE: Tracks the share of 1,664 firms with "any employee ownership" and 8,242 firms with "no employee ownership," as observed in 1999, that were no longer observed in ensuing years.

SOURCE: Data are from USDOL Form 5500 pension database, matched to Standard and Poor's Compustat data on publicly traded companies in the United States, 1999–2010.

lar in Panel B for firms with and without ESOPs and in Panel C for firms where the share of the firm owned by employees is above and below 5 percent.

REGRESSION RESULTS

In Table 4.2, we summarize the hazard ratios from Cox proportional hazard regressions predicting the likelihood of firm disappearance (based on more detailed regression results in Appendix Table 4A.1). For each EO measure, we report the hazard ratios both from the model

Figure 4.1 (continued)

Panel B: Failure rates by ESOP status in 1999

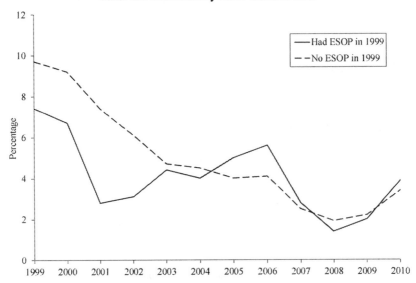

NOTE: Tracks the share of 645 firms with "any ESOPs" and 9,262 firms with "no ESOPs," as observed in 1999, that were no longer observed in ensuing years.

where we treat any disappearance of a firm from the data as a firm failure (column 1) and from the model where we define firm failure strictly as bankruptcy or liquidation (column 2).

Column 1 of Table 4.2 provides strong evidence that EO firms are less likely to disappear than non-EO firms, and the results are statistically significant for all the employee ownership variables in our analysis. As seen in the first entry in column 1, the relative hazard ratio associated with any EO is 0.786 and significant, meaning that EO firms were only 78.6 percent as likely as non-EO companies to disappear in any year over the 1999–2010 period. Second, firms with ESOPs were 82.1 percent as likely as non-ESOP firms to disappear in any year. Third, the value of EO stock per worker was associated with a higher survival probability: an extra $1,000 of employee ownership stock was linked to a 0.5 percent lower risk of disappearing. This means that, since the

Figure 4.1 (continued)

Panel C: Failure rates by EO greater than or less than 5 percent of firm

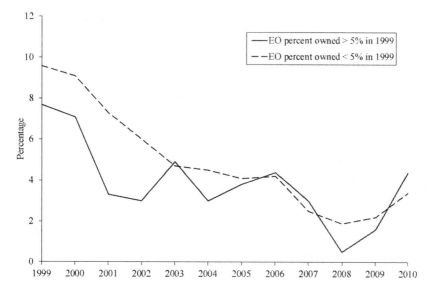

NOTE: Tracks the share of 366 firms with EO percentage of company owned >5% and 9,542 firms with EO percentage of company owned <5%, as observed in 1999, that were no longer observed in ensuing years.

mean value of employee ownership stock among employee owners was $10,613, average employee ownership was linked to a 5.307 percent lower risk of disappearing in any given year. Fourth, the share of the firm owned by employees had a big impact on firm survival: firms where the share of the firm owned by employees was 5 percent or more were only 77.2 percent as likely to disappear as firms with less than a 5 percent share of employee ownership. Finally, the share of workers participating in employee ownership and ESOPs was also negatively related to the likelihood that a firm would disappear: specifically, an increase in the share of the firm's employee owners from 0 percent to 100 percent was associated with a 22.4 percent lower risk of disappearing in any given year, and an increase in ESOP participants at the firm from 0 percent to 100 percent was linked to a 24.4 percent lower risk.

Table 4.2   Summary of the Relationship between Employee Ownership and Firm Survival from Cox Proportional Hazard Regressions Predicting Firm Survival over the Period 1999–2010

	Dependent variable	
	Disappeared for any reason	Disappeared because of bankruptcy or liquidation
Any EO	**0.786**	0.928
ESOP	**0.821**	0.900
EO stock per worker	**0.987**	**0.776**
EO percentage of company owned >5%	**0.772**	0.813
Employee owners as % of all employees	**0.776**	0.800
ESOP participants as % of all employees	**0.756**	0.512

NOTE: Each cell contains the estimated hazard rate from a Cox Proportional Hazard Regression predicting the likelihood of firm death for each EO variable in turn. Full regression results are reported in appendix tables. Each regression controls for firm size, union status, and industry. Bold figures indicate that the hazard estimate is statistically significantly lower than 1.00 ($p < 0.05$).

Turning to column 2 of Table 4.2, using the more stringent firm failure measure of bankruptcy or liquidation, we see that EO firms were less likely than non-EO firms to experience bankruptcy or liquidation in any given year over the 1999–2010 period; however, most of the hazard rates do not achieve statistical significance at the 5 percent level. One important reason for the loss of statistical significance is that the sample size of firms that experienced bankruptcy or liquidation is far smaller than the sample size of those that disappeared from the data set for any reason (only 303 firms over the 1999–2010 period as opposed to 6,100 firms). We therefore are cautious about relying too heavily on this second set of estimates. The only employee ownership measure for which the hazard rate is statistically significant in column 2 is EO stock per worker, which reveals that firms with an extra $1,000 of EO stock were linked to a 22.4 percent lower risk of experiencing bankruptcy or liquidation in any given year during the 1999–2010 period.

To what extent does employment stability mediate or facilitate the positive influence of employee ownership on a firm's likelihood of persisting through negative economic downturns? We investigated whether the positive link between employee ownership and firm survival identified in the above analysis might be partially explained by the employment stability effect of employee ownership. To explore this, we added a control for employment variability to the Cox proportional hazard regression for each employee ownership measure examined above. The idea is to compare the relative hazard ratio in each employee ownership regression before versus after employment variability is controlled for. The employment variability measure we constructed for this purpose is the standard deviation of annual change in the natural log of employment in each company from 1999 to 2010. Appendix Table 4A.2 presents the counterparts of the estimates for firm disappearance for any reason where we also control for employment variability in the Cox proportional hazard regressions. If the relative hazard ratio after controlling for employment variability is closer to one than in the similar specification in column 1 of Table 4.2 that does not control for employment variability, then we can say that employment stability appears to help explain the positive link between employee ownership and firm survival. This is only true in the models where employee ownership is measured by whether the firm has any employee ownership and by the share of workers at the firm participating in employee ownership. In the regressions using the other employee ownership variables, the hazard ratio is further from one than it was in the column 1 specifications from Table 4.2. Therefore, employment stability does not appear to be a major factor in explaining the link between employee ownership and firm survival.

We close this section with a discussion about some caveats. It is important to note that the empirical analysis above does not identify a causal relationship, but simply an observed correlation between employee ownership and firm survival. The fact that employee ownership firms persist for longer periods of time may partially reflect self-selection of both the firms and the workers employed at the EO firms. For example, it may be that employee ownership firms are more likely to self-select into markets or sectors where firm dissolution is more rare; we have tried to address this concern by including industry controls in our hazard regressions. Additionally, there may be self-selection of workers into EO firms in a way that makes these firms more likely to persist. Workers may self-select by unobservable characteristics that can affect firm survival. As Chiaporri and Salanié (2003) point out, a combination of unobserved heterogeneity and endogenous matching of agents to employment contracts can create selection based on the parameters of interest. For example, if more productive or motivated workers are drawn to work at firms that share wealth with their employees through their EO schemes, then these firms may be more likely to succeed during turbulent times.

Alas, selection is a potential threat to identifying a causal relationship in all studies using nonexperimental data (Kremer 1997). Selection bias is most effectively controlled for through random assignment in true experiments. While there have not been any true experiments in the survival of employee ownership firms, it is worth noting that true experiments have been conducted regarding the economic performance effects of group-based incentives, with results indicating causal effects on performance. A randomized field experiment shows favorable effects of firm-based financial incentives on turnover and productivity (Peterson and Luthans 2006). This is complemented by laboratory experiments conducted by Frohlich et al. (1998), who find higher productivity in researcher-designed "employee-owned firms," and by Mellizo (2013), who finds that when subjects are randomly assigned to shared versus individual flat-wage compensation contracts, shared pay motivates higher individual performance, even in the absence of other high-performance workplace practices like decision-making autonomy. While randomized experiments are hard to imagine on the topic of firm survival, these results call out for innovative research strategies to determine the causal role of employee ownership.

CONCLUSION

This chapter has shown that publicly traded companies in the United States with employee ownership programs were more likely to survive the last two recessions. From a research perspective, this is important because it raises questions about the mechanisms and workplace dynamics underlying employee ownership and firm survival, suggesting that employee ownership may affect firm incentives and policies in a way that enhances firm sustainability. It is possible, for example, that employee ownership combines with employee involvement, job training, and job security to create an "ownership culture" that may not only improve short-term performance but also contribute to employee commitment and innovative ideas that enhance long-term survival. We shed more light on this possibility in the next chapter.

From a policy perspective, our finding that firms with employee ownership were more likely to survive these recessions is an important result, because higher survival rates among employee ownership companies could lead to lower job loss rates and unemployment. Employee ownership may therefore serve as an economy-wide policy instrument to lower job loss through increasing the likelihood of firm survival. This indicates positive externalities on the overall economy and government expenditures (e.g., for unemployment compensation and social programs) that would justify supportive public policy, given the large economic and social costs of unemployment resulting from firm closings.

Notes

1. However, it is important to note that recent laboratory experiments conducted by Mellizo (2013) in which subjects are randomly assigned to shared versus individual flat-wage compensation contracts show that shared pay motivates higher individual performance even in the absence of other high-performance workplace practices like decision-making autonomy.
2. We also tested probit models predicting firm death, and these had a similar pattern and strength of results.
3. The Cox proportional hazards model specifies that the hazard rate (i.e., the probability of failure) for firm j with characteristics X_j is

$$h(t|X_j) = h_0(t) \times exp(X\beta),$$

and no functional form is imposed on the baseline hazard $h_0(t)$, which is assumed to be the same for all observations. The semiparametric nature of the Cox model makes it more appealing than other hazard models, which make parametric assumptions about the shape of the baseline hazard like the Weibull model. One firm's hazard is thus simply a multiple of another's, with a constant relative hazard ratio given by

$$h(t|X_j) / h(t|X_m) = exp(X\beta) / exp(X_m\beta).$$

Specifications with Weibull survival models also yielded similar results.
4. These figures pertain to firm failure for any reason; figures for failure strictly due to bankruptcy or liquidation appear similar despite the considerably smaller sample sizes.
5. A similar pattern is observed when we compare trajectories by presence of employee ownership in all years during 1999–2010.

Appendix 4A
Tables

Table 4A.1 Relationship between Employee Ownership and Firm Survival: Cox Proportional Hazard Regressions Predicting Firm Survival over 1999–2010

Panel A: Any EO

	(1) Disappeared for any reason	(2) Disappeared for any reason	(3) Disappeared for any reason	(4) Disappeared bec. of bankruptcy or liquidation	(5) Disappeared bec. of bankruptcy or liquidation	(6) Disappeared bec. of bankruptcy or liquidation
Any EO	0.841***	0.752***	0.786***	0.740*	0.743*	0.928
	(0.0290)	(0.0276)	(0.0291)	(0.122)	(0.126)	(0.164)
Employment		0.984***	0.982***		0.929***	0.925***
		(0.00219)	(0.00247)		(0.0236)	(0.0238)
Union pension plan		0.925	0.964		0.939	1.056
		(0.0518)	(0.0551)		(0.256)	(0.301)
Industry controls	No	No	Yes	No	No	Yes
Observations	95,855	82,900	82,900	95,855	82,900	82,900
Number of firms	13,580	12,461	12,461	13,580	12,461	12,461
Number of failures	6,869	6,100	6,100	341	303	303
Time at risk	2.720e + 07	1.890e + 07	1.890e + 07	2.720e + 07	1.890e + 07	1.890e + 07
Log pseudo likelihood	−63,269	−54,310	−54,201	−3,121	−2,669	−2,588

NOTE: Column entries are hazard ratios. Standard errors are clustered by firm. Robust standard errors in parentheses. * significant at the 0.10 level; ** significant at the 0.05 level; *** significant at the 0.01 level.

Panel B: ESOP

	(1)	(2)	(3)	(4)	(5)	(6)
	Disappeared for any reason	Disappeared for any reason	Disappeared for any reason	Disappeared bec. of bankruptcy or liquidation	Disappeared bec. of bankruptcy or liquidation	Disappeared bec. of bankruptcy or liquidation
ESOP	0.801***	0.747***	0.821***	0.585**	0.653	0.900
	(0.0409)	(0.0405)	(0.0453)	(0.155)	(0.177)	(0.258)
Employment		0.984***	0.981***		0.926***	0.924***
		(0.00229)	(0.00257)		(0.0243)	(0.0236)
Union pension plan		0.898*	0.935		0.924	1.053
		(0.0499)	(0.0533)		(0.253)	(0.305)
Industry controls	No	No	Yes	No	No	Yes
Observations	95,855	82,900	82,900	95,855	82,900	82,900
Number of firms	13,580	12,461	12,461	13,580	12,461	12,461
Number of failures	6,869	6,100	6,100	341	303	303
Time at risk	2.720e+07	1.890e+07	1.890e+07	2.720e+07	1.890e+07	1.890e+07
Log pseudo likelihood	−63,272	−54,326	−54,216	−3,120	−2,669	−2,588

NOTE: Robust standard errors in parentheses. * significant at the 0.10 level; ** significant at the 0.05 level; *** significant at the 0.01 level.

Table 4A.1 (continued)

Panel C: EO Stock per Worker

	(1)	(2)	(3)	(4)	(5)	(6)
	Disappeared for any reason	Disappeared for any reason	Disappeared for any reason	Disappeared bec. of bankruptcy or liquidation	Disappeared bec. of bankruptcy or liquidation	Disappeared bec. of bankruptcy or liquidation
EO stock per worker	0.988***	0.985***	0.987***	0.741***	0.743***	0.776***
	(0.00236)	(0.00253)	(0.00243)	(0.0720)	(0.0710)	(0.0681)
Employment		0.983***	0.980***		0.928***	0.927***
		(0.00229)	(0.00256)		(0.0243)	(0.0236)
Union pension plan		0.902**	0.940		1.130	1.305
		(0.0498)	(0.0531)		(0.303)	(0.363)
Industry controls	No	No	Yes	No	No	Yes
Observations	95,240	82,721	82,721	95,240	82,721	82,721
Number of firms	13,562	12,458	12,458	13,562	12,458	12,458
Number of failures	6,821	6,088	6,088	337	302	302
Time at risk	2.702e + 07	1.883e + 07	1.883e + 07	2.702e + 07	1.883e + 07	1.883e + 07
Log pseudo likelihood	−62,775	−54,193	−54,088	−3,060	−2,636	−2,561

NOTE: Robust standard errors in parentheses. * significant at the 0.10 level; ** significant at the 0.05 level; *** significant at the 0.01 level.

Panel D: EO Percent of Company Owned > 5%

	(1)	(2)	(3)	(4)	(5)	(6)
	Disappeared for any reason	Disappeared for any reason	Disappeared for any reason	Disappeared bec. of bankruptcy or liquidation	Disappeared bec. of bankruptcy or liquidation	Disappeared bec. of bankruptcy or liquidation
EO % of company owned >5%	0.807***	0.717***	0.772***	0.602	0.635	0.813
	(0.0640)	(0.0587)	(0.0637)	(0.248)	(0.259)	(0.337)
Employment		0.983***	0.980***		0.925***	0.924***
		(0.00231)	(0.00257)		(0.0246)	(0.0237)
Union pension plan		0.876**	0.920		0.896	1.050
		(0.0485)	(0.0521)		(0.241)	(0.296)
Industry controls	No	No	Yes	No	No	Yes
Observations	95,855	82,900	82,900	95,855	82,900	82,900
Number of firms	13,580	12,461	12,461	13,580	12,461	12,461
Number of failures	6,869	6,100	6,100	341	303	303
Time at risk	2.720e+07	1.890e+07	1.890e+07	2.720e+07	1.890e+07	1.890e+07
Log pseudo likelihood	−63,278	−54,332	−54,217	−3,122	−2,670	−2,588

NOTE: Robust standard errors in parentheses. * significant at the 0.10 level; ** significant at the 0.05 level; *** significant at the 0.01 level.

Table 4A.1 (continued)

Panel E: Employee Owners as Percentage of All Employees

Variables	(1) Disappeared for any reason	(2) Disappeared for any reason	(3) Disappeared for any reason	(4) Disappeared bec. of bankruptcy or liquidation	(5) Disappeared bec. of bankruptcy or liquidation	(6) Disappeared bec. of bankruptcy or liquidation
Employee owners as % of all employees	0.848***	0.727***	0.776***	0.602**	0.596**	0.800
	(0.0379)	(0.0332)	(0.0359)	(0.140)	(0.134)	(0.186)
Employment		0.984***	0.981***		0.929***	0.926***
		(0.00224)	(0.00251)		(0.0234)	(0.0233)
Union pension plan		0.906*	0.946		0.951	1.075
		(0.0505)	(0.0539)		(0.257)	(0.304)
Industry controls	No	No	Yes	No	No	Yes
Observations	95,424	82,899	82,899	95,424	82,899	82,899
Number of firms	13,565	12,461	12,461	13,565	12,461	12,461
Number of failures	6,834	6,100	6,100	339	303	303
Time at risk	2.700e + 07	1.890e + 07	1.890e + 07	2.700e + 07	1.890e + 07	1.890e + 07
Log pseudo likelihood	−62,917	−54,316	−54,207	−3,100	−2,668	−2,588

NOTE: Robust standard errors in parentheses. * significant at the 0.10 level; ** significant at the 0.05 level; *** significant at the 0.01 level.

Panel F: ESOP Participants as Percentage of All Employees

	(1)	(2)	(3)	(4)	(5)	(6)
	Disappeared for any reason	Disappeared for any reason	Disappeared for any reason	Disappeared bec. of bankruptcy or liquidation	Disappeared bec. of bankruptcy or liquidation	Disappeared bec. of bankruptcy or liquidation
ESOP participants as % of all employees	0.706***	0.661***	0.756***	0.291**	0.336**	0.512
	(0.0544)	(0.0507)	(0.0590)	(0.147)	(0.161)	(0.251)
Employment		0.983***	0.980***		0.927***	0.926***
		(0.00230)	(0.00256)		(0.0243)	(0.0234)
Union pension plan		0.889**	0.929		0.936	1.087
		(0.0492)	(0.0527)		(0.253)	(0.309)
Industry controls	No	No	Yes	No	No	Yes
Observations	95,611	82,898	82,898	95,611	82,898	82,898
Number of firms	13,565	12,461	12,461	13,565	12,461	12,461
Number of failures	6,842	6,100	6,100	341	303	303
Time at risk	2.710e + 07	1.890e + 07	1.890e + 07	2.710e + 07	1.890e + 07	1.890e + 07
Log pseudo likelihood	−63,000	−54,325	−54,216	−3,117	−2,667	−2,587

NOTE: Robust standard errors in parentheses. * significant at the 0.10 level; ** significant at the 0.05 level; *** significant at the 0.01 level.

Table 4A.2 Cox Proportional Hazard Estimates of the Role of Employment Stability in Explaining the Relationship between Employee Ownership and Firm Survival

	(1) Disappeared for any reason	(2) Disappeared for any reason	(3) Disappeared for any reason	(4) Disappeared for any reason	(5) Disappeared for any reason	(6) Disappeared for any reason
Any EO	0.802*** (0.0351)					
ESOP		0.780*** (0.0509)				
EO assets per employee			0.985*** (0.00306)			
EO % of company owned >5%				0.698*** (0.0716)		
Employee owners as % of all employees					0.792*** (0.0427)	
ESOP participants as % of all employees						0.693*** (0.0650)
Employment	0.982*** (0.00305)	0.981*** (0.00314)	0.981*** (0.00312)	0.980*** (0.00316)	0.981*** (0.00309)	0.981*** (0.00314)
Union pension	0.981 (0.0654)	0.967 (0.0640)	0.971 (0.0639)	0.947 (0.0623)	0.965 (0.0641)	0.960 (0.0633)
Employment variation	0.987 (0.0247)	0.995 (0.0246)	0.992 (0.0247)	0.996 (0.0246)	0.989 (0.0247)	0.995 (0.0246)
Industry controls	Yes	Yes	Yes	Yes	Yes	Yes

Observations	78,660	78,660	78,488	78,660	78,660	78,659
Number of firms	9,627	9,627	9,626	9,627	9,627	9,627
Number of failures	4,072	4,072	4,064	4,072	4,072	4,072
Time at risk	1.510e + 07	1.510e + 07	1.505e + 07	1.510e + 07	1.510e + 07	1.510e + 07
Log pseudo likelihood	−35,672	−35,677	−35,588	−35,678	−35,675	−35,676

NOTE: Robust standard errors in parentheses. * significant at the 0.10 level; ** significant at the 0.05 level; *** significant at the 0.01 level.

5
Why Do Employee Ownership Firms Have Greater Stability and Survival?

Why are employee ownership firms more likely to be stable and long lived? Two possible explanations are that either greater compensation flexibility or greater productivity in employee ownership firms accounts for their greater stability and survival. This chapter presents evidence on both these explanations. As will be seen, neither of them provides a full explanation of the greater stability and survival, although the evidence suggests support for a refined version of the productivity explanation.

PAY LEVELS AND FLEXIBILITY

There are two possible ways in which employee ownership may provide pay flexibility to the firm in times of financial distress. First, employers' yearly contributions to employee ownership plans may be more flexible than other types of compensation. When sales decline or other types of negative demand shocks occur, the company may contribute less stock (or money to buy stock) to employee accounts in an employee ownership plan. This type of flexibility is no different from the flexibility that employers have in all defined contribution pension plans: the fact that the contribution is made in stock rather than cash (as in a deferred profit-sharing plan) does not affect the perceived cost of labor from the firm's perspective.

A second source of pay flexibility may be linked specifically to employee ownership if the company stock substitutes in whole or part for fixed pay. The total shareholder return (annual dividend and change in company stock value) may be seen as part of employees' annual compensation. In this case, when negative demand shocks occur, the decrease in company stock value provides an automatic pay cut for workers. Since the fixed component of pay would be lower in this circumstance, firms will have less incentive to lay off workers and are likely to have a higher probability of survival.

There is very little prior evidence on the topic of flexibility in pay among employee ownership firms. We explore this with our Form 5500–Compustat data, measuring pay flexibility in four ways. The first two ways consider just the employer's average annual contribution to compensation per employee, measured either as total compensation per employee (which is reported by fewer than one-fourth of all firms in any year) or merely as total pension expenses per employee (reported for all firms). Compensation flexibility in both cases is computed as the standard deviation of compensation per employee at a given firm over the period 1999–2011, after adjusting for annual compensation growth.[1] In Appendix Table 5A.1 we show that there is little statistically significant association between employee ownership and these two measures of flexibility (columns 1 and 2). Not surprisingly, there is more flexibility associated with employee ownership when shareholder returns are included as part of compensation. The third and fourth measures in Table 5A.1 add dividends and stock price changes to the employee-owned stock (columns 3 and 4) and show greater pay flexibility associated with all the employee ownership measures. The coefficients in Panel A indicate that considering shareholder return as part of pay roughly doubles the yearly variation in pay.[2]

Pay Levels

While these last two results point to greater pay risk associated with employee ownership, a key issue in considering the effects of pay flexibility is whether the variable pay substitutes for fixed pay or benefits. If it does not substitute, and instead comes wholly on top of market levels of fixed pay and benefits, then employee ownership firms will not enjoy any cost advantage in hiring or retaining workers when bad times hit. (In economic terms, the marginal cost of labor would be just as high among employee ownership firms as among those without employee ownership.) In addition, employees would not face extra financial risk in their basic compensation, since the pay variability would occur in the above-market component of their compensation.

As reviewed in Chapter 1, past research indicates that employee ownership tends to come on top of market levels of pay. It is rare for employee ownership to be part of wage or benefit concessions, and studies find that employee ownership firms have average base wages that are as high as, or higher than, those in comparable firms without employee ownership. There is also clear evidence that base pay levels do not generally decrease when ESOPs are adopted in public companies (Kim and Ouimet 2014).

Employee ownership also generally comes on top of standard pay among the firms in our data set. We summarize key results in Table 5.1, with more detail in Appendix Table 5A.2. We present estimates that include comparisons both within and between firms (using random-effect specifications) and only within firms (using fixed-effects specifications). The former comparisons answer the question of how employee ownership relates to compensation levels in general, while the latter comparisons answer the question of what types of changes occur in compensation within a firm when employee ownership is increased or decreased. As can be seen in Table 5.1, employee ownership is associated with higher compensation under either type of comparison. The most telling result is found in column 1 of Table 5.1. If employee ownership substitutes for standard pay, then it should be associated with lower levels of pay, excluding pension contributions. It is not—in fact, nonpension pay is positively linked to employee ownership, with figures indicating between 1.4 and 7.4 percent higher pay across three key measures of employee ownership. Column 2 shows that pension contributions are significantly higher (11.6 percent) in companies with employee ownership, and that they increase by an average of 4.4 percent when companies adopt employee ownership. Combining pension and nonpension data, column 3 shows that employee ownership is linked to 4.0 percent higher compensation in general and a 2.1 percent increase within a firm when employee ownership is added to compensation. These pay differentials are strengthened when shareholder returns are considered part of employee compensation, as shown in column 4.

In sum, there is no support for the idea that employee ownership generally substitutes for standard pay or benefits. Given this, there is no plausible mechanism by which increased pay flexibility under employee ownership can lead to increased stability or survival.

Table 5.1 Summary of Results on Pay Levels and Employee Ownership (%)

	Total nonpension compensation per employee	Total pension contribution per employee	Total compensation per employee	Total compensation plus shareholder returns per employee[a]
Average pay difference associated with any employee ownership in firm				
Comparing both across and within firms	**3.5**	**11.6**	**4.0**	**4.5**
Comparing only within firms over time	1.4	4.4	2.1	3.7
Average pay difference associated with 100% of employees covered by employee ownership plan				
Comparing both across and within firms	**7.4**	**20.7**	**8.8**	**8.3**
Comparing only within firms over time	6.1	13.8	7.7	7.0
Average pay difference associated with mean of employee-owned stock per employee ($10,540)				
Comparing both across and within firms	**2.6**	**4.9**	**2.6**	**3.3**
Comparing only within firms over time	2.1	1.6	2.3	2.9

NOTE: Based on results from Appendix Table 5A.2. Results for "comparing both across and within firms" are based on random-effects specifications, and results for "comparing just within firms over time" are based on fixed effects. Figures in bold are based on statistically significant differences at the 95% level.

[a] Column 4 is based on smaller sample than column 3, accounting for lower figures in rows 3 and 4.

PRODUCTIVITY

The greater stability and survival of employee ownership companies may be due in part to higher productivity. This may happen in one of two ways. First, there may be a simple mediation effect if employee ownership leads to higher productivity (through increased effort, cooperation, monitoring of coworkers, attraction of higher-quality workers, etc.) and the higher productivity leads to greater stability and survival. In this case, the effect of employee ownership should disappear when controlling for productivity level. Second, there may be a more complex mechanism through which employee ownership influences survival and stability through productivity: firms that give stock to employees may try to create an employee ownership culture with a greater sense of ownership, and the sense of ownership is contingent on increased job security, since it is difficult to make employees feel like owners when they are just as likely to be laid off as in any other firm. In this case, employee ownership may be linked to greater productivity in general; however, even when firms are suffering productivity problems, they may want to restrict layoffs in order to maintain an ownership culture, so that ownership may have an effect on stability and survival even when the firm undergoes low-productivity years. As reviewed in Chapter 1, prior research strongly supports the idea that employee ownership is linked to higher productivity, on average.

We first add to the prior literature by estimating the relationship between employee ownership and productivity in our sample. To do this, we use a standard specification based on a production function to control for other influences on productivity. In addition, we examine within-firm as well as between-firm variation.[3]

The findings from our data set are consistent with prior results. As summarized in Table 5.2 (with further detail in Appendix Table 5A.6), employee ownership is linked to 2.9 percent higher productivity using both within- and between-firm comparisons, and 2.4 percent higher productivity using only within-firm comparisons, and the former but not the latter comparison can reject a zero effect. Employee ownership is also strongly linked to productivity when measured as stock per employee (a 2.5–2.6 percent increase associated with average stock per employee) or as percentage of employees covered (a 7.8–12.5 percent

Table 5.2 Summary of Results on Productivity Levels and Employee Ownership

	Productivity difference (%)
Average productivity difference associated with any employee ownership in firm	
Comparing both across and within firms	**2.9**
Comparing only within firms over time	2.4
Average productivity difference associated with median level of employee-owned stock per employee ($10,540)	
Comparing both across and within firms	**2.6**
Comparing only within firms over time	**2.5**
Average productivity difference associated with 100% of employees covered by employee ownership plan	
Comparing both across and within firms	**7.8**
Comparing only within firms over time	**12.5**

NOTE: Based on results from Appendix Table 5A.6. Results for "comparing both across and within firms" are based on random-effects specifications, and results for "comparing only within firms over time" are based on fixed effects. Figures in bold are based on statistically significant differences at the 95% level.

increase associated with 100 percent of employees covered). Further results in Appendix Table 5A.6 show that the companies in which employees own less than 3 percent of company stock have stronger productivity increases than the companies with a higher percentage owned, as is consistent with the findings of Kim and Ouimet (2014) that small ESOPs are associated with stronger productivity effects than large ESOPs.

These results make it plausible that higher productivity accounts for the greater stability and survival of employee ownership firms uncovered in the preceding two chapters. To investigate this, we add productivity controls to the benchmark regression models for employment stability from Chapter 3 and for firm survival from Chapter 4. We test for the influence of productivity as a simple mediator in three ways: first by controlling for the prior year's productivity level, then by controlling for the average productivity level of the company, and finally by controlling for the interaction of productivity and employment changes.[4]

Our tests show that there is no simple connection between the productivity of employee ownership firms and their survival or stability.

We do not report a summary table, since the estimated employee ownership effects change very little when controlling for productivity, and the results are easily summarized in the text. We report regression results in Appendix Table 5A.3 and 5A.4. As can be seen in column 2 of Appendix Table 5A.3, higher average productivity predicts a higher likelihood of disappearance for any reason, which probably indicates that high-productivity firms are tempting targets for mergers and acquisitions. Using the stricter definition of firm death (columns 4–6 of Appendix Table 5A.3), higher productivity not surprisingly predicts a lower likelihood of firm death due to bankruptcy or liquidation, although a zero effect can be rejected only for productivity in the prior year.

For our purposes, the important result is that employee ownership remains a statistically significant predictor of greater survival in columns 1 to 3 after controlling for either productivity variable (i.e., comparing the hazard rate for employee ownership in column 1, which does not control for productivity, against the hazard rate for employee ownership in columns 2 and 3, which do have productivity controls). This is true whether employee ownership is measured as the presence of any employee ownership (Panel A), average stock per employee (Panel B), or percentage of employees covered (Panel C). Controlling for productivity likewise has little effect in columns 4 to 6 on the relationship of employee ownership to disappearance due to bankruptcy or liquidation.

A similar exploration of firm employment stability is undertaken in Appendix Table 5A.4. Columns 1 and 4 present regressions equivalent to those in Appendix Table 3A.1 in Chapter 3 but are restricted to firms with complete information for productivity estimates. We compare these to columns 2 and 5, which add the prior year's productivity as a control, and to columns 3 and 6, which add interactions between a firm's average productivity and the demand shocks. The response to recessionary pressures (measured by increases in the unemployment rate) remains lower among employee ownership firms after controlling for the prior year's productivity level (columns 2 and 5). It is possible that the relationship is due to high-productivity firms having smaller responses to recessionary pressures; however, controlling for interactions of unemployment changes with average firm productivity shows that employee ownership continues to be linked to smaller employment cutbacks as the unemployment rate increases (columns 3 and 6).

Therefore, productivity does not explain in a simple way the greater survival and stability of employee ownership firms. It is possible that external factors explain the greater survival and stability—for example, perhaps customers of employee ownership firms are more loyal because of better customer service. It is also possible that internal factors associated with employee ownership are responsible—for example, perhaps employee ownership companies are less likely to have high executive pay and incentives skewed toward excessively risky decisions (such as executive stock options that reward executives for strong gains but do not penalize them for losses).[5]

We can shed some light on why employee ownership firms have greater stability by conducting further tests of the productivity relationship. Employee ownership firms may lay off fewer workers in recessions and instead assign workers to training or other activities that can build skills or long-term productivity. While these activities may not contribute to short-term productivity, they can help maintain a sense of ownership and ownership culture that contribute to long-term productivity and survival. If this is the case, short-term productivity for employee ownership firms should go down in recessions as workers are retained while sales decrease (i.e., the numerator in the productivity measure decreases more than the denominator decreases).

This idea receives strong support, as summarized in Table 5.3, based on coefficients reported in Appendix Table 5A.5. This is based on productivity regressions that interact employee ownership with the unemployment rate, testing whether the relationship of employee ownership to productivity is related to the level of demand in the economy. While Table 5.2 showed that employee ownership is generally associated with higher productivity, Table 5.3 shows that this relationship is contingent on overall demand in the economy. There is a positive main effect on the employee ownership measures but a negative interaction between employee ownership and the unemployment rate, indicating that the relative productivity of employee ownership firms is high when the economy is strong and decreases when the economy is weak, as the employee ownership firms lay off fewer workers. For example, Table 5.3 shows that in a nonrecession year with unemployment at 5.0 percent, employee ownership firms would have a productivity advantage of 2.4–4.0 percent, while in a recession year with 8.0 percent unemployment, their productivity would be 1.0–1.8 percent lower than that

Table 5.3 Summary of Results on Employee Ownership and Productivity in Recession and Nonrecession Years

	Employee ownership productivity difference (in %) in nonrecession year (unempl. = 5%)	Employee ownership productivity difference (in %) in recession year (unempl. = 8%)
Average productivity difference (in %) associated with any employee ownership in firm		
Comparing both across and within firms	4.0	−1.8
Comparing only within firms over time	3.3	−1.0
Average productivity difference (in %) associated with median level of employee-owned stock per employee ($10,540)		
Comparing both across and within firms	3.1	0.9
Comparing only within firms over time	3.6	2.9
Average productivity difference (in %) associated with 100% of employees covered by employee ownership plan		
Comparing both across and within firms	9.5	2.5
Comparing only within firms over time	20.9	16.3

NOTE: Based on coefficients from Appendix Table 5A.5. Results for "comparing both across and within firms" are based on random-effects specifications, and results for "comparing only within firms over time" are based on fixed effects.

of other comparable firms. Measuring employee ownership as average stock per employee or share of employee covered also shows that the productivity advantage of employee ownership firms goes down in recessions.

While there are no direct data available on how employee ownership firms reassign workers when demand decreases, these results combined with the lower layoffs in employee ownership firms support the idea that they are more likely to put workers in training or in other activities that do not contribute to short-term productivity but may build skills that support greater long-term productivity. A complementary explanation concerns the firm's incentive to retain workers with firm-specific skills when demand decreases, given human capital theory's prediction that firms will share in the costs of firm-specific training and thus have an incentive to maintain the relationship in order to recoup those costs. Investing in an employee ownership culture, in which workers are encouraged to cooperate and share information, may be seen as a type of investment in firm-specific skills, since cooperation and information sharing may be contingent on building trust and good relationships in a team environment, and such relationships are firm specific. In other words, companies may not want to disrupt good working relationships, both among coworkers and between managers and employees, by engaging in layoffs when demand declines, since those relationships may be important for higher productivity after demand recovers.

CONCLUSION

This chapter explores the reasons behind the higher survival and stability of employee ownership firms, focusing on the potential roles of pay flexibility and productivity. Pay is found to be more flexible in employee ownership firms only when total shareholder return is counted as part of compensation, but this is not a plausible mechanism for greater stability or survival, given that the employee ownership comes on top of standard pay and benefits. Any increased flexibility comes in above-market compensation, and the firm would not experience labor cost savings when bad times occur.

The relation of productivity to employee ownership is more promising for providing lessons about stability and survival. Consistent with prior evidence, we find that employee ownership is linked to higher productivity on average, when making comparisons both among firms and within firms. The effect of employee ownership on survival and stability, however, is maintained when controlling for productivity levels. The lesson comes from examining the contingent nature of the relationship between productivity and employee ownership: consistent with the lower layoffs of employee ownership firms, they have lower short-term productivity from retaining more workers as the economy worsens. Retaining more workers may help their long-term productivity, by helping to maintain an employee ownership culture through retaining firm-specific skills and relationships that support such a culture. If this interpretation is correct, it suggests there are strong positive externalities from employee ownership because of the fewer layoffs. This helps to decrease unemployment levels in the economy and maintain purchasing power for greater macroeconomic stability under recessionary pressures.

Notes

1. To avoid having inflation and general wage trends contribute to the measured variation, the natural logarithm of compensation per employee was first regressed on year dummies, and flexibility was computed as the within-firm standard deviation of the residuals in firms with at least three observations.
2. Using the data underlying results in Appendix Table 5A.1, EO firms are predicted to have pay variability of 0.08 in the absence of EO, and 0.18 with EO, in column 3, while the predicted pay variability in column 4 is 0.41 in the absence of EO and 0.81 with EO.
3. We use a translog specification, with industry and year effects, and both fixed-effects and random-effects models. The estimating equation is

$$(1) \quad Ln(Q/L) = (\beta_l - 1) \times Ln(L_{it}) + \beta_k \times Ln(K)_{it} + \beta_{ll} \times [Ln(L_{it}) \times Ln(L_{it})] +$$

$$\beta_{kk} \times [Ln(K_{it}) \times Ln(K_{it})] + \beta_{kl} \times [Ln(L_{it}) \times Ln(K_{it})] +$$

$$\beta_p \times EO_{it} + \beta_d \times DB_{it} + \beta_{dt} \times DC_{it} +$$

$$\beta_{ind} \times (\text{industry dummies}) + \beta_y \times (\text{year dummies}) + u_i + e_{it} \,,$$

where Q = output, defined as sales + inventory change
L = total employees
K = capital stock
EO = employee ownership
DB = defined benefit plan
DC = defined contribution plan
ß = coefficients
u = firm-level fixed or random effect
e = error term
subscript i = firm i, t = year t

4. To generate the productivity variables, a regression based on the productivity
model in endnote 3 was run without the employee ownership and pension variables, and with 12 year dummies and 72 industry dummies as controls. Average
productivity is calculated as the average within-firm residual, and productivity last
year is calculated as last year's residual.

5. There is no available research on executive pay in employee ownership companies, which is a valuable topic for new research.

Appendix 5A

Tables

Table 5A.1 Pay Flexibility and Employee Ownership

Dependent variable:	Std. dev. (ln of total compensation per employee)	Std. dev. (ln of pension contributions per employee)	Std. dev. (ln of total comp. + EO shareholder returns per employee)	Std. dev. (ln of pension contrib. + EO shareholder returns per employee)
		Panel A		
Any EO lasting full period	0.004	0.006	0.100***	0.403***
	(0.013)	(0.015)	(0.016)	(0.017)
n	1,013	4,609	1,231	4,294
R-squared	0.295	0.041	0.353	0.174
		Panel B		
Average EO stock per employee	0.000	0.001	0.005***	0.012***
	(0.000)	(0.001)	(0.000)	(0.001)
n	1,248	5,664	1,502	5,308
R-squared	0.267	0.044	0.352	0.113
		Panel C		
Average % of employees with EO	−0.004	0.006	0.119***	0.572***
	(0.015)	(0.018)	(0.018)	(0.022)
n	1,238	5,645	1,494	5,295
R-squared	0.267	0.044	0.311	0.171

Panel D

Average % of firm owned by employees

>0% and <=1%	0.015	0.023*	0.034**	0.252***
	(0.012)	(0.013)	(0.014)	(0.016)
>1% and <=3%	0.006	0.004	0.052***	0.425***
	(0.014)	(0.017)	(0.016)	(0.020)
>3% and <=5%	0.004	0.081***	0.107***	0.475***
	(0.019)	(0.026)	(0.022)	(0.031)
>5% and <=10%	0.006	0.012	0.131***	0.519***
	(0.018)	(0.026)	(0.021)	(0.030)
>10%	0.028	0.028	0.235***	0.672***
	(0.024)	(0.036)	(0.029)	(0.043)
n	1,211	5,341	1,494	5,289
R-squared	0.276	0.044	0.333	0.197

NOTE: Standard errors in parentheses. * significant at the 0.10 level; ** significant at the 0.05 level; *** significant at the 0.01 level. Based on OLS regressions of pay variability measures on EO measures. Each panel represents results of separate regressions. Control variables include average ln(firm size), average presence of defined benefit plans, average presence of defined contributions plans, plus 71 two-digit industry dummies. Std. dev. = standard deviation; EO = employee ownership; ln = natural logarithm. Standard deviation is calculated only for firms with three or more pay observations over the 1999–2011 period.

Table 5A.2 Pay Levels and Employee Ownership

Dependent variable:	Ln(total compensation per employee)		Ln(pension contributions per employee)		Ln(total compensation excluding pension contributions per employee)		Ln(total compensation + EO shareholder returns per employee)		Ln(pension contributions + EO shareholder returns per employee)	
	Random effects	Fixed effects	Random effects	Fixed effects	Random effects	Fixed effects	Random effects	Fixed effects	Random effects	Fixed effects
Panel A										
Any EO	0.039***	0.021*	0.110***	0.043**	0.034***	0.014	0.044***	0.036**	0.288***	0.111***
	(0.012)	(0.012)	(0.015)	(0.018)	(0.011)	(0.012)	(0.015)	(0.017)	(0.020)	(0.027)
Number of firm-year obs.	14,626	12,619	52,619	45,527	14,334	12,356	12,157	10,286	42,282	35,753
Number of firms	2,007	1,888	7,092	6,772	1,978	1,861	1,871	1,750	6,529	6,088
Panel B										
Average EO stock per employee	0.002***	0.002***	0.005***	0.001**	0.002***	0.002***	0.003***	0.003***	0.030***	0.027***
	(0.000)	(0.000)	(0.001)	(0.001)	(0.000)	(0.000)	(0.000)	(0.000)	(0.001)	(0.001)
Number of firm-year obs.	14,568	12,561	52,494	45,405	14,280	12,303	12,111	10,241	42,202	35,674
Number of firms	2,007	1,887	7,089	6,769	1,977	1,859	1,870	1,748	6,528	6,083
Panel C										
% of employees with EO	0.084***	0.074***	0.188***	0.129***	0.071***	0.059***	0.080***	0.068***	0.363***	0.127***
	(0.015)	(0.016)	(0.020)	(0.023)	(0.014)	(0.015)	(0.018)	(0.020)	(0.026)	(0.035)
Number of firm-year obs.	13,582	11,593	49,952	42,909	13,291	11,331	11,211	9,361	40,283	33,807
Number of firms	1,989	1,853	7,043	6,676	1,960	1,826	1,850	1,714	6,476	5,967

Panel D

% of firm owned by employees										
>0% and <=1%	0.024	0.020	0.112***	0.050**	0.019	0.008	0.063***	0.070***	0.228***	0.149***
	(0.015)	(0.015)	(0.017)	(0.020)	(0.014)	(0.014)	(0.018)	(0.020)	(0.023)	(0.031)
>1% and <=3%	0.067***	0.052***	0.161***	0.053**	0.058***	0.040***	0.058***	0.038*	0.312***	0.059*
	(0.016)	(0.016)	(0.019)	(0.022)	(0.015)	(0.015)	(0.019)	(0.021)	(0.027)	(0.035)
>3% and <=5%	0.053***	0.029	0.128***	0.024	0.046***	0.018	0.045**	0.009	0.343***	0.008
	(0.018)	(0.018)	(0.024)	(0.027)	(0.017)	(0.017)	(0.022)	(0.024)	(0.034)	(0.043)
>5% and <=10%	0.037**	0.010	0.109***	-0.021	0.030*	0.000	-0.023	-0.072***	0.558***	0.154***
	(0.019)	(0.019)	(0.027)	(0.030)	(0.017)	(0.018)	(0.022)	(0.025)	(0.038)	(0.049)
>10%	0.051**	0.031	0.087***	-0.028	0.045**	0.021	0.043	0.009	0.541***	0.027
	(0.023)	(0.024)	(0.034)	(0.038)	(0.021)	(0.022)	(0.028)	(0.032)	(0.050)	(0.065)
Number of firm-year obs.	13,247	11,341	47,073	40,490	13,040	11,160	11,536	9,697	40,628	34,157
Number of firms	1,906	1,770	6,583	6,221	1,880	1,745	1,839	1,705	6,471	5,974

NOTE: Standard errors in parentheses. * significant at the 0.10 level; ** significant at the 0.05 level; *** significant at the 0.01 level. Based on panel regressions with random or fixed firm effects, and AR(1) correction. Panels A to D represent results of separate regressions. Control variables include ln(employment), presence of defined benefit plans, presence of defined contribution plans, plus 12 year dummies and 71 two-digit industry dummies. EO = employee ownership; ln = natural logarithm.

Table 5A.3 Productivity and Firm Survival

Dependent variable:	Disappeared for any reason			Disappeared because of bankruptcy or liquidation		
Panel A						
Any EO	−0.352***	−0.354***	−0.351***	0.173	0.179	0.135
	(0.045)	(0.045)	(0.045)	(0.197)	(0.197)	(0.196)
Average productivity		0.056**			−0.104	
		(0.022)			(0.121)	
Productivity in prior year			0.003			−0.194***
			(0.016)			(0.056)
Number of firms Observations	54,983	54,983	55,818	54,983	54,983	55,818
Panel B						
Average EO stock per employee	−0.022***	−0.022***	−0.022***	−0.211**	−0.210**	−0.216**
	(0.004)	(0.004)	(0.004)	(0.087)	(0.087)	(0.089)
Average productivity		0.057**			−0.105	
		(0.022)			(0.113)	
Productivity in prior year			0.003			−0.181***
			(0.016)			(0.054)
Observations	54,872	54,872	55,706	54,872	54,872	55,706

Panel C

% of employees with EO	-0.415***	-0.418***	-0.410***	0.092	0.103	0.054
	(0.058)	(0.058)	(0.058)	(0.255)	(0.256)	(0.254)
Average productivity		0.057**			-0.103	
		(0.022)			(0.120)	
Productivity in prior year			0.004			-0.192***
			(0.016)			(0.055)
Observations	54,983	54,983	55,818	54,983	54,983	55,818

NOTE: Standard errors in parentheses. * significant at the 0.10 level; ** significant at the 0.05 level; *** significant at the 0.01 level. Based on Cox survival regressions. Panels A, B, and C represent results of separate regressions. Control variables include employment, bargaining status, and nine industry dummies. EO = employee ownership.

132

Table 5A.4 Productivity and Firm Stability

	(1)	(2)	(3)	(4)	(5)	(6)	(7)	(8)	(9)
Negative demand shock: UR increase	−0.02790***	−0.02778***	−0.02797***	−0.028***	−0.028***	−0.028***	−0.028***	−0.028***	−0.028***
	(0.00137)	(0.00137)	(0.00139)	(0.001)	(0.001)	(0.002)	(0.001)	(0.001)	(0.001)
Positive demand shock: UR decrease	0.11089***	0.11094***	0.11157***	0.113***	0.113***	0.114***	0.113***	0.113***	0.113***
	(0.00710)	(0.00711)	(0.00717)	(0.008)	(0.008)	(0.008)	(0.007)	(0.007)	(0.007)
Productivity in prior year		0.01997***			0.020***			0.020***	
		(0.00522)			(0.005)			(0.005)	
Negative shock interacted with:									
EO assets per employee	0.00070***	0.00068***	0.00070***						
	(0.00010)	(0.00010)	(0.00010)						
EO share of employees				0.009***	0.009***	0.009***			
				(0.003)	(0.003)	(0.003)			
ESOP share of employees							0.018***	0.018***	0.018***
							(0.004)	(0.004)	(0.004)
Average firm productivity			0.00083			0.001			0.001
			(0.00238)			(0.002)			(0.002)
Positive demand shock interacted with:									
EO assets per employee	0.00084*	0.00078*	0.00087**						
	(0.00043)	(0.00043)	(0.00043)						
EO share of employees				−0.002	−0.003	−0.002			
				(0.015)	(0.015)	(0.015)			

	(1)	(2)	(3)	(4)	(5)	(6)	(7)	(8)
ESOP share of employees						−0.006 (0.020)	−0.006 (0.020)	−0.007 (0.020)
Average firm productivity		−0.01023 (0.01235)			−0.010 (0.012)			−0.010 (0.012)
Observations	54,881	54,881	54,881	54,983	54,983	54,983	54,983	54,983
R-squared	0.20139	0.20245	0.20143	0.201	0.203	0.202	0.203	0.202
Number of firms	8,900	8,900	8,900	8,902	8,902	8,902	8,902	8,902

NOTES: Dependent variable = change in ln(employment), UR = unemployment rate. Robust standard errors in parentheses. * significant at the 0.10 level; ** significant at the 0.05 level; *** significant at the 0.01 level. Based on fixed-effects panel regressions with controls as reported in Table 3A.1. Each column represents a separate regression.

Table 5A.5 Productivity and Employee Ownership in Recessions

Dependent variable:	Ln[(sales + inventory change)/employees]	
	Random effects (1)	Fixed effects (2)
Panel A		
Any EO	0.134***	0.102***
	(0.026)	(0.026)
Unemployment rate	−0.021***	−0.025***
	(0.002)	(0.002)
Any EO × unemployment rate	−0.019***	−0.014***
	(0.004)	(0.004)
Number of firm-year obs.	70,124	59,689
Number of firms	10,435	9,122
Panel B		
Average EO stock per employee last year	0.006***	0.005***
	(0.001)	(0.001)
Unemployment rate	−0.024***	−0.027***
	(0.002)	(0.002)
Avg. EO stock last year × unemployment rate	−0.001***	−0.000
	(0.000)	(0.000)
Number of firm-year obs.	62,280	52,695
Number of firms	9,585	8,332
Panel C		
% of employees with EO	0.201***	0.255***
	(0.040)	(0.041)
Unemployment rate	−0.022***	−0.023***
	(0.002)	(0.002)
% of employees with EO × unemployment rate	−0.022***	−0.013**
	(0.006)	(0.006)
Number of firm-year obs.	67,753	57,367
Number of firms	10,386	9,038

NOTE: Standard errors in parentheses. * significant at the 0.10 level; ** significant at the 0.05 level; *** significant at the 0.01 level. Based on panel regressions with random or fixed firm effects, and AR(1) correction. Panels A to C represent results of separate regressions. Based on translog specification, with control variables including ln(employment) alone and squared, ln(capital stock) alone and squared, ln(employment) × ln(capital stock), presence of defined benefit plans, presence of defined contribution plans, plus time trend and 71 two-digit industry dummies. EO = employee ownership; ln = natural logarithm.

Table 5A.6 Productivity and Employee Ownership

Dependent variable:	Ln[(sales + inventory change)/employees]	
	Random effects	Fixed effects
Panel A		
Any EO	0.029**	0.024
	(0.013)	(0.016)
Number of firm-year obs.	70,124	59,689
Number of firms	10,435	9,122
Panel B		
Average EO stock per employee	0.002***	0.002***
	(0.001)	(0.001)
Number of firm-year obs.	62,280	52,695
Number of firms	9,585	8,332
Panel C		
% of employees with EO	0.075***	0.118***
	(0.019)	(0.021)
Number of firm-year obs.	67,753	57,367
Number of firms	10,386	9,038
Panel D		
% of firm owned by employees		
>0% and <=1%	0.037**	0.033*
	(0.016)	(0.018)
>1% and <=3%	0.036*	0.045**
	(0.019)	(0.021)
>3% and <=5%	0.028	0.022
	(0.023)	(0.026)
>5% and <=10%	0.020	0.009
	(0.026)	(0.029)
>10%	0.023	0.005
	(0.033)	(0.036)
Number of firm-year obs.	62,628	53,160
Number of firms	9,468	8,245

NOTE: Standard errors in parentheses. * significant at the 0.10 level; ** significant at the 0.05 level; *** significant at the 0.01 level. Based on panel regressions with random or fixed firm effects, and AR(1) correction. Panels A to D represent results of separate regressions. Based on translog specification, with control variables including ln(employment) alone and squared, ln(capital stock) alone and squared, ln(employment) × ln(capital stock), presence of defined benefit plans, presence of defined contribution plans, plus 12 year dummies and 71 two-digit industry dummies. EO = employee ownership; ln=natural logarithm.

6
Conclusions and Policy Implications

In this final chapter, our goal is to bring together all the evidence we have presented in this book to make a case for why broad-based employee ownership is appealing, discuss the policy case for employee ownership, and present a list of concrete policy recommendations that can increase the prevalence of employee ownership in our society.

Broad-based sharing in company ownership and in the rewards of economic prosperity has a long and rich history in the United States, with roots that can be traced to the philosophies of the founding fathers. As described in Chapter 2, George Washington's Treasury secretary, Alexander Hamilton, was a proponent of share schemes and advanced a bill, which Congress passed in 1792 and Washington signed into law, that strengthened share schemes in the cod fishing industry. Thomas Jefferson's Treasury secretary, Albert Gallatin, spearheaded a profit-sharing plan in 1795 in his Philadelphia Glass Works company because he believed such a system was important for the newly developing U.S. democracy. With a similar motive, Thomas Jefferson greatly expanded the size of the United States through the Louisiana Purchase with the goal of increasing opportunities for broad-based ownership of land, and this goal was later realized through the Homestead Act. Broadening the distribution of wealth was a key underlying driver for the creation of employee stock ownership plans (ESOPs) and their institutionalization through the Employee Retirement Income Security Act of 1974 (ERISA), spearheaded by Louisiana senator Russell Long.

Interest in employee ownership can be categorized into four main sources, as described in Chapter 1:

1) Increased economic performance

2) Greater job security and firm survival

3) More-broadly shared prosperity

4) Less labor-management conflict and higher quality of work life

Our findings in this book are focused on the second source of interest—job security and firm survival—but also shed light on the issues of

137

economic performance and broadly shared prosperity. Using matched Form 5500–Compustat longitudinal data on the universe of publicly traded firms in the United States from 1999 to 2011, we have examined how firms with employee ownership programs weathered the recessions of 2001 and 2008 relative to firms without employee ownership programs. Our key results are that

- employee ownership firms exhibit greater employment stability in the face of economy-wide and firm-specific shocks (Chapter 3) and

- employee ownership firms had greater survival likelihood in the face of recession, with a lower likelihood of failure (bankruptcy or liquidation) or of disappearance because of mergers and acquisitions (Chapter 4).

- These findings are not explained by greater compensation flexibility or lower wages in employee ownership firms; in fact, employee ownership tends to come on top of base pay that is higher, and no more variable, than in other firms. Productivity is higher on average in employee ownership firms, and the pattern across the business cycle suggests a plausible explanation for the stability and survival results: the productivity advantage of employee ownership firms drops during recessions, indicating that they may retain more workers as a way to facilitate long-term productivity and survival by helping maintain firm-specific human capital and working relationships (Chapter 5). While workplace culture may also help to explain the greater survival of employee ownership firms, we do not have enough information to provide a strong explanation for the increased survival.

Overall, these results imply that at a macroeconomic level, employee ownership may play a role in decreasing unemployment and helping to stabilize the economy under recessionary pressures.

One interesting question is which dimensions of employee ownership contribute the most to stability and survival. Throughout the book, we have described the potential benefits of employee ownership on workplace culture: it can contribute to an environment that promotes higher productivity, greater stability, and higher rates of survival. We do not have measures of workplace culture in this data set, so we cannot draw conclusions on its importance. In comparing the different measures of employee ownership, we find that stability and survival are linked to greater degrees of employee ownership as measured by employer stock per employee, percentage of company owned by employees, and share of employees who are employee owners. While each of these is important, the greatest explanatory power comes from the share of employees who are employee owners, which is the variable most consistent with the idea that it is a cooperative workplace rather than direct financial incentives that drive the improved productivity, stability, and survival.[1]

LIMITATIONS AND IMPLICATIONS FOR FUTURE RESEARCH

As in all nonexperimental research, we cannot fully resolve the issue of causality. It may be that firms that are more stable or have a higher likelihood of survival are more likely to adopt employee ownership, or that there are other unobserved factors—such as management quality or philosophy, or use of other high-performance work policies—that explain the relationship. Even if other factors are responsible for the stability and survival, it is nonetheless noteworthy that these are accompanied by employee ownership, indicating that employee ownership may be used to reinforce the stability and survival prospects. In addition, there is a plausible story that employee ownership plays a direct role based on the finding that the productivity advantage of employee ownership firms disappears in recessions as they hold onto workers, possibly as a way of maintaining an ownership culture and retaining firm-specific skills. The evidence is clear that employee ownership is associated with higher productivity on average, but this has not been studied across the business cycle. While laboratory and field experiments that control for selection and other biases have shed light on the productivity effects and financial incentives of employee ownership (Frohlich et al. 1998; Mellizo 2013; Peterson and Luthans 2006), it is difficult to conceive of an experiment that tests the employment stability and survival effects of employee ownership. A promising method of examining the possible causal mechanisms would be to combine additional analysis of large data sets with in-depth case studies of how employee ownership firms cope with recessions.

One advantage of our data is that we have the entire population, rather than just a sample, of U.S. publicly traded companies over the 1999–2011 period. This means that we do not have to worry about generalizing our results to the population for this period; however, there is still uncertainty about generalizing the results of this period to future periods, and to firms without employee ownership if they were somehow induced or made to adopt employee ownership. If some of the public policies discussed below were implemented and were successful in increasing the adoption of employee ownership, it is possible that these new adopters would not exhibit the same behavior as the employee ownership firms we have studied, because (for example) they may be taking advantage of tax incentives rather than developing an ownership culture that supports stability and survival. There are, however, a number of countries (such as the United Kingdom) where the government implemented tax incentives (Oxera Consulting 2007a,b,c), as discussed earlier in this book, and the findings on firms' responses to these law changes are generally consistent with our findings for the United States in this book.

There is also a question as to how our results from publicly traded firms would generalize to closely held firms.[2] Closely held firms, also known as privately held firms, are firms that are owned by a relatively small number of shareholders or employees and whose shares are not traded on stock market exchanges but, rather, are offered and exchanged privately. The results in this book are consistent with the one existing study on stability and survival among closely held firms with employee ownership (Blasi, Kruse, and Weltmann 2013), but there is a clear need for further research. Closely held firms with employee ownership tend to have a greater share of the firm that is employee owned on average and are more likely than publicly traded firms to be majority owned by employees,[3] which makes them particularly important to study in order to understand the impacts of high levels of employee ownership and the role of a highly concentrated ownership culture in stability, survival, and productivity. The major research difficulty in studying closely held firms is the lack of sufficient data, since little of their information is publicly available.

Finally, our core analysis on employment stability and firm survival is based on data on employee ownership in deferred compensation plans. This is largely a data availability constraint—we use one of the few large data sets available that contain information on employee ownership—namely, the U.S. Department of Labor's Form 5500 pension records. A large portion of employee ownership in the United States occurs through ESOPs, which are covered by Form 5500. Data on direct, broad-based employee ownership at the firm or worker level—through ESOPs, exercised stock options, or open market purchases—are scarce. There is information on compensation composition, including compensation consisting of stock and stock option holdings, available from the Standard and Poor's Compustat Execucomp database, but this focuses only on the top five highest-paid executives at each firm and therefore precludes the analysis of broad-based employee ownership. We believe the collection of large-scale data on all forms of employee ownership holdings within firms would be of tremendous benefit to employee ownership research.

Given the results in this book and the high stakes involved in employment stability and firm survival, there would be a potentially large payoff to further research on employee ownership in both publicly traded and closely held firms.

POLICY JUSTIFICATIONS

Public policies are commonly justified by market failures such as externalities, incomplete information, and public goods. With respect to the second source of interest—greater job security and firm survival—the decision to lay off workers or close a firm can create a number of negative externalities, including

- negative effects on consumer purchasing power and aggregate demand,
- higher government expenditures on unemployment compensation and other forms of support for dislocated workers and economically stressed families,[4]

- potentially harmful effects on communities, such as increased crime and a decreased tax base for supporting schools and infrastructure, and

- potentially harmful social and personal effects, such as marital breakups and alcohol abuse.

These externalities are illustrated by an estimate based on the General Social Survey (GSS) data that the federal government saved $13.7 billion per year in tax revenue and unemployment compensation over the period 2002–2010 because of the lower layoff rates among employee owners (Employee Ownership Foundation 2013; Rosen 2013).

The third source of interest in employee ownership—more-broadly shared prosperity—can also be seen as a form of positive externality that may justify supportive public policy. Raising the incomes of middle- and lower-class workers can help mitigate the increasing inequality of income and wealth. Extreme inequality may pose dangers to the viability of a representative democracy, as was believed by several of the founding fathers and argued recently by Stiglitz, among others. Stiglitz (2013a,b) has also made the case that inequality is harmful to macroeconomic growth and stability. This is supported by OECD studies that have found that countries with increasing inequality had slower growth, are more prone to recessions, and had more severe responses to the 2008 crisis.[5] The greater economic stability in more equal societies may be due to more purchasing power in the hands of middle- and lower-class citizens. In addition, low incomes and high inequality are linked to a variety of economic and social problems, including reduced educational performance, mental and physical health problems, teenage births, incarceration, and decreased economic prospects and social mobility for one's children (Wilkinson and Pickett 2010). The evidence presented here is consistent with prior evidence that employee ownership tends to come on top of other pay and wealth, indicating that it can play a role in improving incomes across the economic spectrum.

The first and fourth sources of interest in employee ownership— 1) increased economic performance and 4) less labor-management conflict and higher quality of work life—do not generally involve externalities, since most of the gains should be captured by the participating firms and workers (although there may be some positive externalities such as increased innovation that create wider benefits, and higher economic performance and lower conflict may contribute to employment growth and stability, which have positive effects on the economy as a whole).[6] If employee ownership helps to create higher productivity and better quality of work life, this should provide good private incentives for firms to adopt employee ownership, as well as for workers to join such firms. There may nonetheless be a case for supportive public policy based upon information problems or institutional barriers that limit the adoption of employee ownership. The "public good" nature of information means that there can be a role for government to improve economic performance by spreading information on best practices. This is a common role for government; examples include the long history of agricultural extension services through land-grant universities (since 1887) to spread information on best practices in farming, and employer education conducted by the Occupational Safety and Health Administration on safety practices that can decrease employer costs and improve firm performance by reducing turnover and lost work time from injuries and illnesses.

In sum, employee ownership can improve individual firm performance, and this provides a case for firms to adopt these performance-enhancing practices. The government can play a valuable role in spreading this information. Furthermore, there is a strong case for supportive public policy of employee ownership if employee ownership firms lay off fewer workers and are more likely to survive, because of the negative externalities of layoffs and firm failures that are borne by workers, families, communities, and the larger economy and society. In addition, a policy case can be built on increasing broad-based prosperity, which can reduce inequality and strengthen democracy.

POLICY RECOMMENDATIONS

The European Union (EU) highlighted employee ownership and profit sharing in its four reports from 1991 to 2008 on Promotion of Employee Participation in Profits and Enterprise Results (the "Pepper Reports"), including a summary of the variety of fiscal and tax incentives provided by EU countries for employee ownership, stock options, and profit sharing in its 2008 report. The United States has had a variety of incentives for ESOPs since the 1980s, though some were eliminated during the first Bush administration.[7] Employer contributions to ESOPs are tax deductible, but that is the case for all eligible pension plans. The major surviving tax incentive specific to employee ownership is the ability for retiring owners to avoid capital gains taxes if they sell to an ESOP owning at least 30 percent of the company.

Past experience has shown that government legislation promoting employee ownership can increase the adoption and use of employee ownership schemes. This was true with tax advantages for firms that have ESOPs in the United States, tax incentives to individuals for employee ownership in the United Kingdom, and tax advantages to firms and individuals for profit sharing in France, among other examples. There is a positive correlation between supportive legislation and prevalence, making a case that government backing and support can be effective.

So what are some concrete policy recommendations that can lead to increased prevalence of broad-based employee share ownership in our society? In what follows, we present a list of policy options. The empirical analysis in this book has focused on the population of U.S. firms that are publicly traded on the stock market, and many of the policy options below have special relevance to publicly traded firms. However, there are several options that will encourage closely held companies, also. In particular, options 1, 2, 3, and 5, below, will likely have the biggest impact on publicly traded firms, while the other options will be relevant for both publicly traded and closely held companies.

We start our list of recommendations with tax and expenditure policies that our results suggest may be justified by positive externalities such as lower unemployment. Such policy options include the following seven:

1) Inducing financial firms to invest in or loan money to firms with broad-based employee ownership. Financial institutions could deduct a portion of the interest income from loans to employee ownership firms. This policy existed in the 1980s, but despite its success in stimulating interest among financial institutions, the program was cut back as part of deficit-reduction measures.

2) Restricting tax deductibility of incentive pay for top executives (stock, bonuses, stock options) to companies that have a

similar type of incentive for all employees. This would make incentive plans subject to the same conditions that exist for pensions and health insurance plans: they are tax deductible only if they are broad based, not limited to a small group. This would not prevent firms from having special incentive plans for top executives, but would simply establish that such plans should not be given tax privileges.

3) Making a minimal program of employee ownership a precondition for the numerous corporate tax incentives in the tax code. This is in the spirit of George Washington's tax credit for cod fishing ships that required a profit-sharing plan for any ships benefiting from the credit.

4) Expanding eligibility for exemption from capital gains taxes for retiring owners selling to an ESOP. Currently, this is not available to S corporations, which have been rapidly growing in the past decade.[8]

5) Extending tax deductibility from deferred to nondeferred employee ownership plans. At present, the United States only provides tax incentives for deferred employee ownership plans through the ERISA law of 1974. Federal legislation could provide tax breaks to firms that provide direct broad-based employee ownership of stock and stock options.

6) Requiring or favoring firms with broad-based ownership plans in government procurement. The federal government currently spends large sums procuring goods and services from companies. These firms that hold federal contracts are already subject to certain special laws—for example, laws that govern diversity. The U.S. government could require federal contractors to incorporate broad-based employee ownership for doing business with the federal government (for example, based on the objective scorecard proposed in point 12, below).

7) Having federal, state, and local economic development authorities give special attention to firms with broad-based equity ownership programs in awarding tax abatements to businesses for social improvement projects.

Apart from the tax and expenditure policies, there are a number of policies to spread information or break down institutional barriers that limit adoption; these low-cost policies can be justified under each of the reasons for interest in employee ownership. Policies that spread information include these five:

8) Establishing a national commission to "assess different inclusive capitalist initiatives and evaluate ways to improve and promote them in American society" (Blasi, Freeman, and Kruse 2013, p. 198). The United States has often used commissions to draw attention and expertise to national issues.

9) Establishing an office to support broad-based capitalism within the White House, reviewing public policies and working with the private sector to publicize and encourage best practices.

10) Providing seed grants to establish employee ownership resource centers in each state, modeled on the successful centers in Ohio and Vermont that assist local businesses with transitions to employee ownership and provide ongoing technical assistance, support, and networking.

11) Establishing programs in the Small Business Administration to educate owners of small- and medium-sized businesses about employee ownership options and to work with state programs in providing assistance to firms in creating employee ownership trusts to buy out retiring owners.

12) Creating an objective scorecard of employee ownership and profit sharing that can be used by workers, investors, and government officials in measuring the spread of these programs in individual firms and throughout the economy. This would include common measures of the percentages of employees covered by different types of plans, and the size and distribution of their financial stakes in these plans.

A final low-cost idea offered here involves expanding state policies to allow firms with financial participation to form and operate more easily:

13) In the United States, firms incorporate at the state level, and states can amend their laws on corporations to create legal forms that make it easier for firms to make decisions consis-

tent with the goal of broadening financial participation. Since 2010, 28 states have passed laws creating a new type of corporation, called the B corporation (short for "Benefit corporation"), which makes it easier for businesses to take employee, community, and environmental interests into consideration when making decisions.[9] A firm with broad-based employee ownership incorporated as a B corporation has greater options to maintain its programs than a firm incorporated under different provisions.

CONCLUSION

Combining our findings with the empirical literature as a whole, we see a body of evidence showing that, despite the theoretical free-rider and financial risk objections raised against it, employee ownership is generally linked to increased worker performance and commitment, enhanced employee cooperation toward firm goals, lower turnover, higher pay, and wealth, as well as to improved firm-level outcomes such as higher productivity, greater employment stability, and firm survival. These benefits—particularly the greater stability and survival, which can help the overall economy by reducing unemployment and resisting recessionary pressures—can provide a clear justification for widespread government support to broaden employee ownership programs.

Notes

1. The t- and z-statistics are higher on employee owners as a percentage of all employees, compared to the other measures, indicating that this employee ownership variable explains a greater share of the variance in stability and survival. This conclusion is reinforced by the finding that the magnitudes of moving from no employee ownership to high levels of employee ownership are larger for this variable.
2. Relatedly, our analysis of publicly traded companies skews our sample toward large and historically successful companies.
3. "The median percentage ownership for ESOPs in public firms is about 5 percent. . . . The median percentage ownership for private firms is about 30–50 percent, with

about 4,000 companies now 100 percent employee-owned by ESOPs (a percentage that is increasing steadily)." See NCEO (2016).

4. Unemployment Insurance is experience rated so that employers with higher levels of layoffs pay more into the system, but the payments are not directly proportional, so that employers do not absorb the full costs of the UI for workers they dismiss.

5. See Aiginger and Guger (2012); OECD (2016).

6. See Brill (2012) on how S corporation ESOPs may justify favorable tax treatment by contributing to higher economic growth in both recession and nonrecession periods.

7. A federal law that was instituted in 1984 with strong bipartisan support, Internal Revenue Code Section 133 gave tax incentives to banks and financial institutions lending money to companies to set up ESOPs. Specifically, the lender was able to deduct from its corporate taxes half of its interest income on the loan to set up the ESOP. Section 133 provided a strong incentive for setting up ESOPs at corporations, but it was substantially repealed during the first Bush administration in a wave of deficit-reduction initiatives.

8. A bipartisan bill has been introduced to extend this tax treatment to S corporations. See http://esca.us/2016/04/press-release-esca-members-to-testify-today-at-house -committee-on-small-business-hearing-on-s-esops/.

9. The purpose of a B corporation includes creating general public benefit, which is defined as a material positive impact on society and the environment. A B corporation's directors and officers operate the business with the same authority as in a traditional corporation but are required to consider the impact of their decisions not only on shareholders but also on society and the environment. The B corporation can refuse to sell itself to the highest bidder, can operate with a longer-term financial horizon, and can value interests beyond maximizing shareholder wealth, in ways that other corporations cannot easily do.

References

Aiginger, Karl, and Alois Guger. 2012. "Stylized Facts on the Interaction between Income Distribution and the Great Recession." Paper presented at the NERO meeting of OECD, held in Paris, June 18. http://www.oecd.org/eco/Inequality%20depth%20of%20crisis%20paper.pdf (accessed November 30, 2016).

Akerlof, George A. 1982. "Labor Contracts as Partial Gift Exchange." *Quarterly Journal of Economics* 97(4): 543–569.

Arando, Saioa, Monica Gago, Derek C. Jones, and Takao Kato. 2015. "Efficiency in Employee-Owned Enterprises: An Econometric Case Study of Mondragon." *Industrial and Labor Relations Review* 68(2): 398–425.

Arellano, Manuel, and Stephen Bond. 1991. "Some Tests of Specification for Panel Data: Monte Carlo Evidence and an Application to Employment Equations." *Review of Economic Studies* 58(2): 277–297.

Axelrod, Robert. 1984. *The Evolution of Cooperation.* New York: Basic Books.

Babenko, Ilona, and Rik Sen. 2014. "Money Left on the Table: An Analysis of Participation in Employee Stock Purchase Plans." *Review of Financial Studies* 27(12): 3658–3698.

Becker, Brian E., and Mark A. Huselid. 1998. "High-Performance Work Systems and Firm Performance: A Synthesis of Research and Managerial Implications." In *Research in Personnel and Human Resources*, Vol. 16, Gerald R. Ferris, ed. Greenwich, CT: JAI Press, pp. 53–101.

Ben-Ner, Avner. 1988. "The Life Cycle of Worker-Owned Firms in Market Economies: A Theoretical Analysis." *Journal of Economic Behavior and Organization* 10(3): 287–313.

Blair, Margaret, Douglas L. Kruse, and Joseph R. Blasi. 2002. "Employee Ownership: An Unstable Form or a Stabilizing Force?" In *The New Relationship: Human Capital in the American Corporation*, Margaret Blair and Thomas Kochan, eds. Washington, DC: Brookings Institution Press, pp. 241–289.

Blasi, Joseph R., Michael Conte, and Douglas L. Kruse. 1996. "Employee Ownership and Corporate Performance among Public Corporations." *Industrial and Labor Relations Review* 50(1): 60–79.

Blasi, Joseph R., Richard B. Freeman, and Douglas L. Kruse. 2013. *The Citizen's Share: Putting Ownership Back into Democracy.* New Haven, CT: Yale University Press.

———. 2016. "Do Employee Ownership, Profit Sharing, and Broad-Based Stock Options Help the Best Firms Do Even Better?" *British Journal of Industrial Relations* 54(1): 55–82.

Blasi, Joseph R., Richard B. Freeman, Christopher Mackin, and Douglas L. Kruse. 2010. "Creating a Bigger Pie? The Effects of Employee Ownership, Profit Sharing, and Stock Options on Workplace Performance." In *Shared Capitalism at Work: Employee Ownership, Profit and Gain Sharing, and Broad-Based Stock Options*, Douglas L. Kruse, Richard B. Freeman, and Joseph B. Blasi, eds. Chicago: University of Chicago Press, pp. 139–165.

Blasi, Joseph R., Maya Kroumova, and Douglas L. Kruse. 1997. *Kremlin Capitalism: The Privatization of the Russian Economy*. Ithaca, NY: Cornell University Press.

Blasi, Joseph R., and Douglas L. Kruse. 1991. *The New Owners: The Mass Emergence of Employee Ownership in Public Companies and What It Means to American Business*. New York: HarperCollins.

Blasi, Joseph R., Douglas L. Kruse, and Dan Weltmann. 2013. "Firm Survival and Performance in Privately Held ESOP Companies." In *Sharing Ownership, Profits, and Decision-Making in the 21st Century*, Douglas L. Kruse, ed. Vol. 14 in the series Advances in the Economic Analysis of Participatory and Labor-Managed Firms, Takao Kato, ed. Bingley, UK: Emerald Group Publishing, pp. 109–124.

Bova, Francesco, Yiwei Dou, and Ole-Kristian Hope. 2015. "Employee Ownership and Firm Disclosure." *Contemporary Accounting Research* 32(2): 639–673.

Brill, Alex. 2012. *An Analysis of the Benefits S ESOPs Provide the U.S. Economy and Workforce*. Washington, DC: Matrix Global Advisors.

Brown, Sarah, Fathi Fakhfakh, and John G. Sessions. 1999. "Absenteeism and Employee Sharing: An Empirical Analysis Based on French Panel Data, 1981–1991." *Industrial and Labor Relations Review* 52(2): 234–251.

Bryson, Alex, and Richard B. Freeman. 2010. "How Does Shared Capitalism Affect Economic Performance in the United Kingdom?" In *Shared Capitalism at Work: Employee Ownership, Profit and Gain Sharing, and Broad Based Stock Options*, Douglas Kruse, Richard Freeman, and Joseph Blasi, eds. Chicago: University of Chicago Press, pp. 201–224.

Buchele, Robert, Douglas Kruse, Loren Rodgers, and Adria Scharf. 2010. "Show Me the Money: Does Shared Capitalism Share the Wealth?" In *Shared Capitalism at Work: Employee Ownership, Profit Sharing, Gainsharing, and Broad-Based Stock Options*, Douglas L. Kruse, Richard B. Freeman, and Joseph R. Blasi, eds. Chicago: University of Chicago Press, pp. 351–375.

Burdin, Gabriel. 2014. "Are Worker-Managed Firms More Likely to Fail than Conventional Enterprises? Evidence from Uruguay." *Industrial and Labor Relations Review* 67(1): 202–238.

Burdin, Gabriel, and Andres Dean. 2009. "New Evidence on Wages and

Employment in Worker Cooperatives Compared with Capitalist Firms." *Journal of Comparative Economics* 34(4): 517–533.

Chiaporri, Pierre Andre, and Bernard Salanié. 2003. "Testing Contract Theory: A Survey of Some Recent Work." In *Advances in Economics and Econometrics*, Vol. 1, Mathias Dewatripont, Lars Peter Hansen, and Stephen J. Turnovsky, eds. Cambridge: Cambridge University Press, pp. 115–149.

Craig, Ben, John Pencavel, Henry Farber, and Alan Krueger. 1995. "Participation and Productivity: A Comparison of Worker Cooperatives and Conventional Firms in the Plywood Industry." *Brookings Papers on Economic Activity: Microeconomics* 1995(1): 121–174.

Cramton, Peter, Hamid Mehran, and Joseph S. Tracy. 2008. "ESOP Fables: The Impact of Employee Stock Ownership Plans on Labor Disputes." Staff Report No. 347. New York: Federal Reserve Board of New York. https://www.newyorkfed.org/medialibrary/media/research/staff_reports/sr347.pdf (accessed June 3, 2016).

Deller, Steven, Ann Hoyt, Brent Hueth, and Reka Sundaram-Stukel. 2009. *Research on the Economic Impact of Cooperatives*. Madison, WI: University of Wisconsin Center for Cooperatives. http://reic.uwcc.wisc.edu/sites/all/REIC_FINAL.pdf (accessed October 3, 2016).

DeVaro, Jed, and Fidan Ana Kurtulus. 2010. "An Empirical Analysis of Risk, Incentives, and the Delegation of Worker Authority." *Industrial and Labor Relations Review* 63(4): 641–661.

Doucouliagos, Chris. 1995. "Worker Participation and Productivity in Labor-Managed and Participatory Capitalist Firms: A Meta-Analysis." *Industrial and Labor Relations Review* 49(1): 58–77.

Dube, Arindrajit, and Richard B. Freeman. 2010. "Complementarity of Shared Compensation and Decision-Making Systems: Evidence from the American Labor Market." In *Shared Capitalism at Work*, Douglas L. Kruse, Richard B. Freeman, and Joseph R. Blasi, eds. Chicago: University of Chicago Press, pp. 167–200.

Earle, John S., and Saul Estrin. 1998. "Workers' Self-Management in Transitional Economies." In *Advances in the Economic Analysis of Participatory and Labor-Managed Firms*, Vol. 6, Will Bartlett and Milica Uvalic, eds. Bingley, UK: Emerald Group Publishing, pp. 3–28.

Employee Ownership Foundation. 2013. "Research Indicates ESOPs Save Federal Government Billions Due to Fewer Layoffs." Press release, January 14. Washington, DC: Employee Ownership Foundation. http://www.esopassociation.org/news-landing/2013/01/14/research-indicates-esops-save-federal-government-billions-due-to-fewer-layoffs (accessed June 3, 2016).

Fakhfakh, Fathi, Virginie Pérotin, and Monica Gago. 2012. "Productivity,

Capital, and Labor in Labor-Managed and Conventional Firms: An Investigation on French Data." *Industrial and Labor Relations Review* 65(4): 847–879.

Fehr, Ernst, and Simon Gächter. 2000. "Cooperation and Punishment in Public Goods Experiments." *American Economic Review* 90(4): 980–994.

Freeman, Richard B., Douglas L. Kruse, and Joseph R. Blasi. 2010. "Worker Responses to Shirking under Shared Capitalism." In *Shared Capitalism at Work: Employee Ownership, Profit and Gain Sharing, and Broad-Based Stock Options*, Douglas L. Kruse, Richard B. Freeman, and Joseph R. Blasi, eds. Chicago: University of Chicago Press, pp. 77–104.

Freeman, Steven F. 2007. "Effects of ESOP Adoption and Employee Ownership: Thirty Years of Research and Experience." Organizational Dynamics Working Paper No. 07-01. Philadelphia: University of Pennsylvania.

Frohlich, Norman, John Godard, Joe A. Oppenheimer, and Frederick A. Starke. 1998. "Employee versus Conventionally Owned and Controlled Firms: An Experimental Analysis." *Managerial and Decision Economics* 19(4–5): 311–326.

Fudenberg, Drew, and Eric Maskin. 1986. "The Folk Theorem in Repeated Games with Discounting or with Incomplete Information." *Econometrica* 54(3): 533–554.

Gintis, Herbert, Samuel Bowles, Robert Boyd, and Ernst Fehr, eds. 2005. *Moral Sentiments and Material Interests: The Foundations of Cooperation in Economic Life*. Cambridge, MA: MIT Press.

Hansen, Daniel G. 1997. "Worker Performance and Group Incentives: A Case Study." *Industrial and Labor Relations Review* 51(1): 37–49.

Hansmann, Henry. 1996. *The Ownership of Enterprise*. Cambridge, MA: Harvard University Press.

Hashi, Iraj, and Alban Hashani. 2013. "Determinants of Financial Participation in the EU: Employers' and Employees' Perspectives." In *Sharing Ownership, Profits, and Decision-Making in the 21st Century*, Douglas L. Kruse, ed. Vol. 14 in the series Advances in the Economic Analysis of Participatory and Labor-Managed Firms, Takao Kato, ed. Bingley, UK: Emerald Group Publishing, pp. 187–215.

Holmstrom, Bengt, and Paul Milgrom. 1994. "The Firm as an Incentive System." *American Economic Review* 84(4): 972–991.

Ichniowski, Casey, Thomas Kochan, David Levine, Craig Olson, and George Strauss. 1996. "What Works at Work: Overview and Assessment." *Industrial Relations* 35(3): 299–333.

Ichniowski, Casey, Kathryn Shaw, and Giovanna Prennushi. 1997. "The Effects of Human Resource Management Practices on Productivity: A Study of Steel Finishing Lines." *American Economic Review* 87(3): 291–313.

Jensen, Michael C., and William H. Meckling. 1992. "Specific and General Knowledge and Organizational Structure." In *Contract Economics*, Lars Werin and Hans Wijkander, eds. Oxford: Blackwell Publishers, pp. 251–274.

Jones, Derek C., Panu Kalmi, Takao Kato, and Mikko Makinen. 2013. "Performance Pay and Worker Separation: A Duration Analysis of Finnish Linked Employer-Employee Data." Paper presented at the Society for the Advancement of Socio-Economics Twenty-Fifth Annual Conference, "States in Crisis," held in Milan, Italy, June 27–29.

Jones, Derek C., and Takao Kato. 1995. "The Productivity Effects of Employee Stock-Ownership Plans and Bonuses: Evidence from Japanese Panel Data." *American Economic Review* 85(3): 391–414.

Kaarsemaker, Eric. 2006. *Employee Ownership and Its Consequences: Synthesis-Generated Evidence for the Effects of Employee Ownership and Gaps in the Research Literature.* York, UK: University of York.

Kaarsemaker, Eric, Andrew Pendleton, and Erik Poutsma. 2010. "Employee Share Ownership Plans: A Review." In *The Oxford Handbook of Participation in Organizations*, Adrian Wilkinson, Paul J. Gollan, Mick Marchington, and David Lewin, eds. Oxford: Oxford University Press, pp. 315–337.

Kachalina, Tatiana. 2013. "Employee Ownership in Russia: Evolution and Current Status." In *Sharing Ownership, Profits, and Decision-Making in the 21st Century*, Douglas L. Kruse, ed. Vol. 14 in the series Advances in the Economic Analysis of Participatory and Labor-Managed Firms, Takao Kato, ed. Bingley, UK: Emerald Group Publishing, pp. 159–185.

Kardas, Peter, Adria L. Scharf, and Jim Keogh. 1998. "Wealth and Income Consequences of ESOPs and Employee Ownership: A Comparative Study from Washington State." *Journal of Employee Ownership Law and Finance* 10(4): 3–52.

Kim, E. Han, and Paige Ouimet. 2014. "Broad-Based Employee Stock Ownership: Motives and Outcomes." *Journal of Finance* 69(3): 1273–1319.

Kremer, Michael. 1997. "Why Are Worker Cooperatives So Rare?" NBER Working Paper No. 6118. Cambridge, MA: National Bureau of Economic Research.

Kroumova, Maya. 2000. "Investment in Employer Stock through 401(k) Plans: Is There Reason for Concern?" PhD dissertation. New Brunswick, NJ: Rutgers University.

Kruse, Douglas, and Joseph Blasi. 1997. "Employee Ownership, Employee Attitudes, and Firm Performance: A Review of the Evidence." In *The Human Resources Management Handbook, Part 1*, David Lewin, Daniel J. B. Mitchell, and Mahmood A. Zaidi, eds. Greenwich, CT: JAI Press, pp. 131–151.

———. 1999. "Public Opinion Polls on Employee Ownership and Profit Sharing." *Journal of Employee Ownership Law and Finance* 11(3): 3–25.

Kruse, Douglas L., Joseph R. Blasi, and Rhokeun Park. 2010. "Shared Capitalism in the U.S. Economy: Prevalence, Characteristics, and Employee Views of Financial Participation in Enterprises." In *Shared Capitalism at Work: Employee Ownership, Profit and Gain Sharing, and Broad-Based Stock Options*, Douglas L. Kruse, Richard B. Freeman, and Joseph R. Blasi, eds. Chicago: University of Chicago Press, pp. 41–75.

Kruse, Douglas L., Richard B. Freeman, and Joseph R. Blasi. 2010. "Do Workers Gain by Sharing? Employee Outcomes under Employee Ownership, Profit Sharing, and Broad-Based Stock Options." In *Shared Capitalism at Work: Employee Ownership, Profit and Gain Sharing, and Broad-Based Stock Options*, Douglas L. Kruse, Richard B. Freeman, and Joseph R. Blasi, eds. Chicago: University of Chicago Press, pp. 257–289.

Kurtulus, Fidan Ana, and Douglas L. Kruse. 2016. "How Did Employee Ownership Firms Weather the Last Two Recessions? Employee Ownership and Employment Stability in the U.S.: 1999–2011." Department of Economics Working Paper. Amherst: University of Massachusetts Amherst.

Kurtulus, Fidan Ana, Douglas Kruse, and Joseph Blasi. 2011. "Worker Attitudes towards Employee Ownership, Profit Sharing, and Variable Pay." In *Advances in the Economic Analysis of Participatory and Labor-Managed Firms*, Vol. 12, Jed DeVaro, ed. Bingley, UK: Emerald Group Publishing, pp. 143–168.

Levine, David, and Richard Parkin. 1994. "Work Organization, Employment Security, and Macroeconomic Stability." *Journal of Economic Behavior and Organization* 24(3): 251–271.

Long, Richard, and John Shields. 2005. "Performance Pay in Canadian and Australian Firms: A Comparative Study." *International Journal of Human Resource Management* 16(10): 1783–1811.

Markowitz, Harry, Joseph Blasi, and Douglas Kruse. 2010. "Employee Stock Ownership and Diversification." *Annals of Operations Research* 176(1): 95–107.

McCarthy, John E., Paula Voos, Adrienne E. Eaton, Douglas L. Kruse, and Joseph R. Blasi. 2011. "Solidarity and Sharing: Unions and Shared Capitalism." In *Employee Ownership and Shared Capitalism: New Directions in Research*, Ed Carberry, ed. Ithaca, NY: Cornell University Press, pp. 27–57.

Mellizo, Phil. 2013. Can Group Incentives without Participation Survive the Free-Rider Problem? A View from the Lab." In *Sharing Ownership, Profits, and Decision-Making in the 21st Century*, Douglas L. Kruse, ed. Vol. 14 in the series Advances in the Economic Analysis of Participatory and Labor-Managed Firms, Takao Kato, ed. Bingley, UK: Emerald Group Publishing, pp. 27–59.

Milgrom, Paul, and John Roberts. 1990. *Economics, Organization, and Management.* New York: Prentice Hall.

Mygind, Niels, Natalia Demina, Aleksandra Gregoric, and Rostislav Kapelyushnikov. 2006. "Corporate Governance Cycles during Transition: A Comparison of Russia and Slovenia." *Corporate Ownership and Control* 3(4): 52–64.

National Center for Employee Ownership (NCEO). 2016. *A Detailed Overview of Employee Ownership Plan Alternatives.* Oakland, CA: National Center for Employee Ownership. http://www.nceo.org/articles/comprehensive -overview-employee-ownership (accessed November 30, 2016).

O'Boyle, Ernest H., Pankaj C. Patel, and Erik Gonzalez-Mulé. Forthcoming. "Employee Ownership and Firm Performance: A Meta-Analysis." *Human Resource Management Journal.*

Olsen, Erik. 2013. "The Relative Survival of Worker Cooperatives and Barriers to Their Creation." In *Sharing Ownership, Profits, and Decision-Making in the 21st Century,* Douglas L. Kruse, ed. Vol. 14 in the series Advances in the Economic Analysis of Participatory and Labor-Managed Firms, Takao Kato, ed. Bingley, UK: Emerald Group Publishing, pp. 83–108.

Organisation for Economic Co-operation and Development (OECD). 2016. *Growth and Inequality: A Close Relationship?* Paris: Organisation for Economic Co-operation and Development. http://www.oecd.org/economy/ growth-and-inequality-close-relationship.htm (accessed November 30, 2016).

Oxera Consulting. 2007a. *Tax-Advantaged Employee Share Schemes: Analysis of Productivity Effects; Report 1: Productivity Measured Using Turnover.* HM Revenue and Customs Research Report No. 32. London: Her Majesty's Revenue and Customs.

———. 2007b. *Tax-Advantaged Employee Share Schemes: Analysis of Productivity Effects; Report 2: Productivity Measured Using Gross Value Added.* HM Revenue and Customs Research Report No. 33. London: Her Majesty's Revenue and Customs.

———. 2007c. *Tax-Advantaged Employee Share Schemes: Analysis of Productivity Effects; Overview.* HM Revenue and Customs Research Report No. 33. London: Her Majesty's Revenue and Customs.

Park, Rhokeun, Douglas L. Kruse, and James Sesil. 2004. "Does Employee Ownership Enhance Firm Survival?" In *Employee Participation, Firm Performance, and Survival,* Virginie Pérotin and Andrew Robinson, eds. Vol. 8 in the series Advances in the Economic Analysis of Participatory and Labor-Managed Firms, Takao Kato, ed. Bingley, UK: Emerald Group Publishing, pp. 3–33.

Pateman, Carole. 1970. *Participation and Democratic Theory.* Cambridge: Cambridge University Press.

Peach, Eric Krassoi, and T. D. Stanley. 2009. "Efficiency Wages, Productivity, and Simultaneity: A Meta-Regression Analysis." *Journal of Labor Research* 30(3): 262–268.

Pencavel, John, and Ben Craig. 1992. "The Behavior of Worker Cooperatives: The Plywood Companies of the Pacific Northwest." *American Economic Review* 82(5): 1083–1105.

———. 1994. "The Empirical Performance of Orthodox Models of the Firm: Conventional Firms and Worker Cooperatives." *Journal of Political Economy* 102(4): 718–744.

Pencavel, John, Luigi Pistaferri, and Fabiano Schivardi. 2006. "Wages, Employment and Capital in Capitalist and Worker-Owned Firms." *Industrial and Labor Relations Review* 60(1): 23–44.

Pendleton, Andrew, Keith Whitfield, and Alex Bryson. 2009. "The Changing Use of Contingent Pay in the Modern British Workplace." In *The Evolution of the Modern Workplace*, William Brown, Alex Bryson, John Forth, and Keith Whitfield, eds. Cambridge: Cambridge University Press, pp. 256–284.

Pérotin, Virginie. 1987. "Conditions of Survival and Closure of French Worker Cooperatives: Some Preliminary Findings." In *Advances in the Economic Analysis of Participatory and Labor-Managed Firms*, Vol. 2, Derek C. Jones and Jan Svejnar, eds. Greenwich, CT: JAI Press.

———. 1997. "What Makes Co-ops Work? Institutional Viability, Firm Creation, Survival, and Closure among Workers' Cooperatives in France." PhD dissertation. Ithaca, NY: Cornell University.

———. 2004. "Early Cooperative Survival: The Liability of Adolescence." In *Employee Participation, Firm Performance, and Survival*, Virginie Pérotin and Andrew Robinson, eds. Vol. 8 in the series Advances in the Economic Analysis of Participatory and Labor-Managed Firms, Takao Kato, ed. Bingley, UK: Emerald Group Publishing, pp. 67–86.

Pérotin, Virginie, and Andrew Robinson. 2002. "Employee Participation in Profit and Ownership: A Review of the Issues and Evidence." Paper prepared for the European Parliament. Leeds, UK: Leeds University Business School.

Peterson, Suzanne J., and Fred Luthans. 2006. "The Impact of Financial and Nonfinancial Incentives on Business-Unit Outcomes over Time." *Journal of Applied Psychology* 91(1): 156–165.

Pierce, Jon L., Stephen A. Rubenfeld, and Susan Morgan. 1991. "Employee Ownership: A Conceptual Model of Process and Effects." *Academy of Management Journal* 16(1): 121–144.

Prendergast, Canice. 2002. "The Tenuous Tradeoff between Risk and Incentives." *Journal of Political Economy* 110(5): 1071–1102.

Rosen, Corey. 2013. "The Impact of Employee Ownership and ESOPs on Lay-offs and the Costs of Unemployment to the Federal Government." Oakland, CA: National Center for Employee Ownership. http://www.nceo.org/assets/pdf/articles/EO_Costs_of_Unemployment.pdf (accessed June 3, 2016).

Scharf, Adria, and Christopher Mackin. 2000. "Census of Massachusetts Companies with Employee Stock Ownership Plans (ESOPs)." Boston: Commonwealth Corp.

Stiglitz, Joseph. 2013a. *The Price of Inequality: How Today's Divided Society Endangers Our Future*. New York: W. W. Norton and Co.

———. 2013b. "Inequality Is Holding Back the Recovery." *New York Times*, January 19. http://opinionator.blogs.nytimes.com/2013/01/19/inequality-is-holding-back-the-recovery/ (accessed October 11, 2016).

Thomas, Alan, and Chris Cornforth. 1989. "The Survival and Growth of Worker Co-operatives: A Comparison with Small Businesses." *International Small Business Journal* 8(1): 34–50.

U.S. Department of Labor (USDOL). 2015. *Private Pension Plan Bulletin: Abstract of 2012 Form 5500 Annual Reports*. Washington, DC: U.S. Department of Labor, Employee Benefits Security Administration.

U.S. General Accounting Office (USGAO). 1986. "Employee Stock Ownership Plans: Benefits and Costs of ESOP Tax Incentives for Broadening Stock Ownership." GAO/PEMD-87-8. Washington, DC: General Accounting Office.

U.S. Senate. 1939. *Survey of Experiences in Profit Sharing and Possibilities of Incentive Taxation*. Hearings before a subcommittee of the Committee on Finance, United States Senate, 75th Cong., 3rd sess., pursuant to S. Res. 215, providing for an investigation of existing profit-sharing systems between employers and employees in the United States, November 21 to December 14, 1938. Washington, DC: Government Printing Office.

Weiss, Andrew. 1987. "Incentives and Worker Behavior." In *Incentives, Cooperation, and Risk Sharing*, Haig Nalbantian, ed. Totowa, NJ: Rowman and Littlefield, pp. 137–150.

Weitzman, Martin L. 1984. *The Share Economy*. Cambridge, MA: Harvard University Press

Welbourne, Theresa M., and Linda A. Cyr. 1999. "Using Ownership as an Incentive: Does the 'Too Many Chiefs' Rule Apply in Entrepreneurial Firms?" *Group and Organization Management* 24(4): 438–460.

Weltmann, Dan, Joseph R. Blasi, and Douglas L. Kruse. 2015. "Does Employee Ownership Affect Attitudes and Behaviors? The Role of Selection, Status, and Size of Stake." In *Advances in the Economic Analysis of Participatory and Labor-Managed Firms*, Vol. 16, Antti Kauhanen, ed. Bingley, UK: Emerald Group Publishing, pp. 249–275.

Wilkinson, Richard, and Kate Pickett. 2010. *The Spirit Level: Why Greater Equality Makes Societies Stronger*. New York: Bloomsbury Press.

Authors

Fidan Ana Kurtulus is an associate professor of economics at the University of Massachusetts Amherst, a Wertheim Fellow at Harvard Law School, a research fellow at the Institute for the Study of Labor (IZA), and a research coordinator for the LERA Employment Policy Research Network. She earned a doctoral degree in economics from Cornell University. The Upjohn Institute for Employment Research awarded her an Early Career Research Award in 2012–2013. Her research explores a number of topics in labor economics, including the organization of workers within firms, participatory workplace practices and employee ownership, the causes and consequences of workplace diversity, and the long-term effects of affirmative action legislation on the U.S. employment landscape since the civil rights movement. She has published in such journals as *Industrial and Labor Relations Review, Industrial Relations*, the *Journal of Policy Analysis and Management*, and the *Annals of the American Academy of Political and Social Science.*

Douglas L. Kruse is a distinguished professor of economics at Rutgers School of Management and Labor Relations, a research associate with the National Bureau of Economic Research, a research fellow at the Institute for the Study of Labor (IZA), an editor of the *British Journal of Industrial Relations*, and director of the Rutgers Program for Disability Research. He earned his doctorate in economics from Harvard University. He conducts econometric studies on employee ownership, profit sharing, disability, worker displacement, pensions, and wage differentials. In 2013–2014, he served as a senior economist at the White House Council of Economic Advisers. His previous book for the Upjohn Institute, *Profit Sharing: Does It Make a Difference?*, won Princeton University's Richard A. Lester Award for the Outstanding Book in Industrial Relations and Labor Economics of 1993. His most recent coauthored books include *The Citizen's Share: Reducing Inequality in the 21st Century* (Yale University Press), *People with Disabilities: Sidelined or Mainstreamed?* (Cambridge University Press), and *Shared Capitalism at Work* (University of Chicago Press). He has published widely in journals such as *Industrial and Labor Relations Review, Economic Journal, Human Resource Management, Monthly Labor Review*, and *Industrial Relations.*

Index

Note: Italic letters *f, t,* and *n* following a page number indicate a figure, table, or note. EO is an abbreviation for "employee ownership."

161

About the Institute

The W.E. Upjohn Institute for Employment Research is a nonprofit research organization devoted to finding and promoting solutions to employment-related problems at the national, state, and local levels. It is an activity of the W.E. Upjohn Unemployment Trustee Corporation, which was established in 1932 to administer a fund set aside by Dr. W.E. Upjohn, founder of The Upjohn Company, to seek ways to counteract the loss of employment income during economic downturns.

The Institute is funded largely by income from the W.E. Upjohn Unemployment Trust, supplemented by outside grants, contracts, and sales of publications. Activities of the Institute comprise the following elements: 1) a research program conducted by a resident staff of professional social scientists; 2) a competitive grant program, which expands and complements the internal research program by providing financial support to researchers outside the Institute; 3) a publications program, which provides the major vehicle for disseminating the research of staff and grantees, as well as other selected works in the field; and 4) an Employment Management Services division, which manages most of the publicly funded employment and training programs in the local area.

The broad objectives of the Institute's research, grant, and publication programs are to 1) promote scholarship and experimentation on issues of public and private employment and unemployment policy, and 2) make knowledge and scholarship relevant and useful to policymakers in their pursuit of solutions to employment and unemployment problems.

Current areas of concentration for these programs include causes, consequences, and measures to alleviate unemployment; social insurance and income maintenance programs; compensation; workforce quality; work arrangements; family labor issues; labor-management relations; and regional economic development and local labor markets.

CPSIA information can be obtained
at www.ICGtesting.com
Printed in the USA
FFOW05n2014130217

9 780880 995252